Reaching Keet Seel

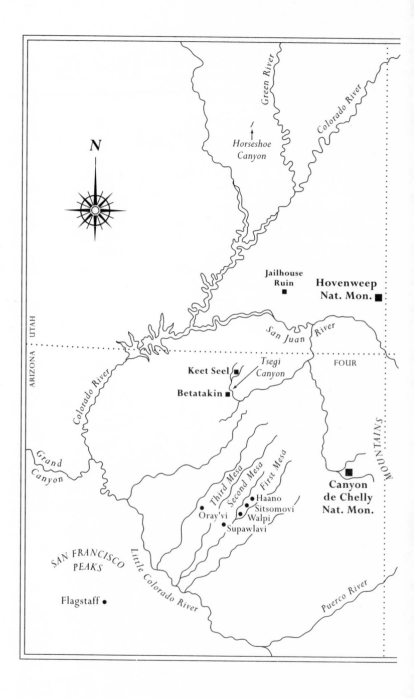

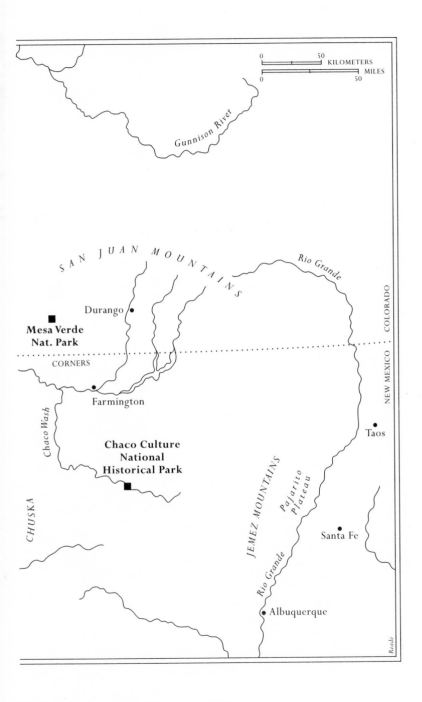

KILOMETERS

MILES

Gunnison River

SAN JUAN MOUNTAINS

Rio Grande

Durango

Mesa Verde
Nat. Park

COLORADO

CORNERS

NEW MEXICO

Chaco Wash

Farmington

Taos

Chaco Culture
National
Historical Park

CHUSKA

JEMEZ MOUNTAINS

Pajarito Plateau

Santa Fe

Rio Grande

Albuquerque

Reade

Reaching Keet Seel

Ruin's Echo and the Anasazi

Reg Saner

The University of Utah Press
Salt Lake City

This book is printed on acid-free, archival-quality paper.

Manufactured in the United States of America

03 02 01 00 99 98 6 5 4 3 2

Illustrations by Sue MacDougall

Library of Congress Cataloging-in-Publication Data

Saner, Reg.
    Reaching Keet Seel : ruin's echo and the Anasazi / Reg Saner.
        p.   cm.
    ISBN 0-87480-553-8 (alk. paper)
        1. Pueblo Indians—Antiquities. 2. Southwest, New—Antiquities.
    3. Southwest, New—Description and travel.   I. Title.
    E99.P9S189   1998
    979'.01—dc21   97-32435

For Tim and Nick,
trail mates.

One thought ever at the fore—
That in the Divine Ship, the World, breasting Time and Space,
All Peoples of the globe together sail, sail the same voyage,
are bound to the same destination.

WALT WHITMAN

Contents

Preface

Among the many and excellent books on those ancient Pueblo peoples called the Anasazi, few or none explore our feelings toward them. Maybe that is reason enough for this book to rest comfortably, if humbly, in your hands. You may already know a lot about the Anasazi, their canyons and mesas, or may have only heard of them. Either way, you are likely to know that archaeological and anthropological treatments of the subject abound, each carrying its own indispensable fascination. But you may also be open to a more personal voice.

"Personal" need not mean uninformed, of course, and in the present case I hope it doesn't. Nonetheless, I've deliberately left most of the archaeological data implied, not spelled out—between the lines, as it were. By setting down what it has felt like to ponder sites evocative of the Anasazi presence, I have explored in this book our living relation—yours and mine—to the most impressive prehistoric culture in North America, one still very much alive among modern Pueblos. In reading time's textures, the Anasazi past made sensually present, we cannot help feeling the story of civilization retold minus writing.

Then, too, there's the influence of terrain. We become what surrounds us, and that is especially true of the peoples we group together under the name "Anasazi." So, because Anasazi culture grew out of an intimate kinship with the high Southwest long before we Euro-Americans began our own incursions there, this book is about both them and their places: the one unimaginable apart from the other.

"Up-and-Down Sun: Notes on the Sacred" begins with the incident that led me to wander in a highly personal way toward a sort of "center place" in ancient Pueblo culture, with "Spirit Root" providing a natural conclusion. Between those two, shorter essays describe points along the way—but in nothing like a straight line. Over more than a dozen summers, with an occasional autumn thrown in, I have fed my pleasure in the ruins, the canyons and mesas of this book, as other work permitted. "Points along the way" were both places and steps toward answering two deceptively simple questions: "Why do I find these things so strangely moving?" and "What are they trying to tell me?"

My last, best wish for these pages is that they may partly evoke, as well, that spellbinding land, so harsh and sincere, with its almost narcotic allure—but without the sunburn, the odd rattler or scorpion, the foot weariness, the juniper midges, and gnat clouds. Elsewhere by armchair has its advantages.

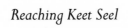

Reaching Keet Seel

If a man settles in a certain place and does not bring forth the fruit of that place, the place itself casts him out, as one who has not borne its fruit.

—Verba Seniorum, ca. A.D. 400

Desert Wisdom

Desert images first came into my life as early as third grade, via a subject Sister Mary Denise told us was "Bible History." Between the ocher covers of our text were lots of pictures. Naturally, to a seven-year-old they seemed a good thing.

Our copies even had pictures on the outsides: bearded and sandal-wearing people in long gowns, like Arabs, amid tall smudges for palm trees, their black lines half-incised into the cloth binding.

Inside were more date palms, camels, oasis pools, and wilderness thickets looking thorny and sin-stricken. Foregrounded against them, robed figures posed as Solomon, Abraham, and best of all, Goliath, with his bashed forehead, the stone still imbedded. Beside that downed giant, the sling-carrying boy, David, took his humbly victorious stance.

Foregrounded indeed. Throughout those holy stories the desert itself remained a sort of nowhere, within which the chosen people wandered as if in limbo. To those devoted followers trooping after their leader Moses, desert was less than a place you wanted out of; less, because not so much a place as a punishment. For as long as you wandered there, you knew you weren't yet good *enough*. You were nowhere all right, and there "on approval." You just hoped one day God would approve you enough to let you out.

Understandably so. People must eat, and for a whole migration of mouths, those barrens didn't offer much sustenance. From "Bible

History" I recall vividly the pictures of the miracle of manna, heaven sent, just when Moses and his desert-wandering band were famished to the verge of despair. Now, a lifetime later, it seems ironic that the tamarisk tree (sometimes called salt cedar) was brought here from the Middle East, where its cousin, *Tamarix mannifera,* does indeed produce edible oozings called manna.

Though the chosen people fed on manna, my dim little third-grade mind could hardly have seen them as hunter-gatherers like the Tohono O'odham Indians (Papago) or the Apache, much less Anasazi, a name I'd never heard of. Yet the Anasazi, as I was to learn, saw desert not as a place of exile but as home. Whereas the Israelites led by Moses are described in scripture as having spent forty desert-years wandering, the Anasazi spent a thousand. The difference was more than just years. To the Anasazi, each high desert place they went wandering toward became their Promised Land.

A far greater difference, however, lay in how each people saw the rock and sand under their feet.

Wherever lands seemed slow to yield returns, the biblical view of nature was peculiarly combative. *Its* chosen people wrested, leveled, subdued, beat back, beat down, whacked at, tamed, exploited. Always, the land existed insofar as it could be dominated, made to yield. And only that yield was visible. Apart from what it rendered, the land itself wasn't. Not even background. If biblical minds agreed on one thing, it was that desert is demonic. To efface it utterly was to praise the Lord.

Had I lived in those biblical places and times, I'd have felt the same. With nobody able to imagine eras of more people than land, wilderness then was fit only for the devils or malefic spirits thought to inhabit it—along with the occasional outcast.

Lately our minds have undergone complete reversal. Instead of seeing it as accursed, we lend the very emptiness of such regions a sacral aura. Odd that in this universe where maybe nothing is divine except what's missing, our last few desert places seem profoundly blessed by what isn't there. We now feel that truly to bring forth the fruit of such terrain is to agree that its silence and space are unimprovable. We say so any time we answer its hush with an attentive stillness, one wide and deep as respect.

Up-and-Down Sun
NOTES ON THE SACRED

Low cloud stuffed with its own importance. And indeed, at Keams Canyon—as over desert of the Four Corners area generally—it's near the rainy season; season of the Niman ritual, when the Katsina spirits "go home." Past my parked car Hopi men and their families ride in pickups toward the ceremony's focus at First Mesa. They come from points distant and near—Albuquerque, Las Cruces, Phoenix, Tucson, Flagstaff, Prescott. More pickups, Southwestern vehicle of choice, are parked along the road. By my own truck I'm quietly sipping a bottled beer taken cold and dripping from an ice chest. Intermittently, as sun breaks through, I squint at its highlighting of otherwise rather rubbly, glum-colored Keams Canyon rock. Up comes a panhandler, Hopi by the cut of him, a short skinny guy in Western shirt and jeans under the obligatory black Stetson.

"Where you from?" he asks me. His blurry eyes glisten.

"Boulder," I say. "Boulder, Colorado. And you?"

"You're doing fine, aren't you?" he says, looking at my beer.

Foolishly—no, stupidly—I'd forgotten the laws against alcohol on reservations. "Oh. . . ," I say, flustered, realizing that to offer him a beer could be the start of a bigger, more awkward mistake. "Yeah, I'm doing okay. How're you doing?"

"You couldn't let me have a little money, could you? I got no money, but I got to get down the road just the same."

Out of charity and paleface guilt, and why-the-hell-not, I give him two dollars.

"Can you make it three?"

Our eyes meet. I tell him I cannot make it three.

He grows uncertain. Keep working me, or drift on? He drifts. A few vehicles farther down the road he wavers up to a pair of Anglo males standing by their Jeep Cherokee, who give him nothing.

At that sight of what my own culture has done to so spiritual a nation as the Hopi, I feel personally degraded. I could shrug, call it fate or history. I don't call it anything, just feel it: what my kind have inflicted on his kind.

Out of some vague cultural remorse, I don't want to think about who that mooch was before devastation. *Way* before—by many and many a century. But not wanting to means I can't help thinking about it: who he was, would have been; who his ancestors had been long, long before Columbus, an ancestral past mocked by the present. Seven, eight centuries ago his forebears had been among those pre-historic and varied peoples we now call by a collective name, the Anasazi.

To the extent that humankind is one family, they were my ancestors, too, though in a relation more metaphoric than actual. Except for one thing: Anasazi ruins and culture had already held a long-standing fascination for me when I discovered that my habit, year in, year out, of watching the sun rise eastward over our treeless Colorado plain had made me the equivalent of a Hopi or Zuñi sun priest and thus, retrospectively, an Anasazi sun watcher as well.

In one of those illogically logical moments during which we make big decisions, unaware that we have, my chance encounter with a disoriented Pueblo Indian gives rise to a sort of vow. "Next June," I promise myself, "I'm going down to Chaco Canyon for the summer solstice." Instantly, I wonder if I will. Why should I? "Boulder to Chaco," I tell myself, "that's over four hundred miles."

Well, emotion itself is a reason, and mine in this case seems to begin with the sun.

ᔕ

Hopi and Zuñi people hold the moment of sunrise to be sacred, as their Anasazi avatars must have done too. But "sacred" is a translator's term for naming something which that very term gives us to misunderstand: Our Judeo-Christian sense of "sacred" creates assumptions having little relation to what the word inevitably distorts when applied to so-called primitive or archaic beliefs—or does so, if for us "sacred" retains any content at all.

As weighed in the hand of the analytical mind, so wishful a syllable melts like a snowflake, or sifts to emptiness like a fistful of beach sand tightly clenched underwater. The rational self may hear it as one more pious vacuity. Rightly weighed, says the mind, belief always comes down to desire. And the will to believe is a wish, a wish that realities from here to the grave's kingdom come be other than they are.

So it would seem. As to what "sacred" tells us about the speaker, the mind's likeliest guess is that, consciously or not, such a speaker supposes sacrosanct terms do him credit, the mark of a spiritual sort.

ᔕ

"On the other hand," says the mind—and the mind is nothing if not two-handed—"having killed the last god, doesn't your rational materialism find it a lonely old cosmos?"

"Lonely? God, yes!" says mind's other side. "But not lonely enough to invite Him/Her/It back from exile. We couldn't do that. Not without taking leave of mental powers grown so apt at explaining phenomena we first invented gods to account for. Nature explains nature, not some voice from a cloud."

Then an inner voice sounds from far off, far as the start of the mind. "But listen," it calls, out of distant red epochs, and plaintively, as if clad in the rags of old habits, "I simply cannot survive a world where nothing is sacred!" It begs us to forgo reason's naturalizing the supernatural, humanizing the divine.

Thus our dilemma, and then some. Do we give in to what reason says is regressive, however ancestral? Or do we let those cravings go the way of flint knives and hunter-gatherer ideas of the cosmos? And if we do let go, letting such voices die, giving up thumb-sucking —if we at last ship off "the sacred" to some Museum of Archaic Ideas—what then? Even assuming that religious emotions are indeed illusory, is human life possible without them? Their impulses seem so universal as to be innate, as if encoded genetically. Are they evolution's protection against what evolution itself has created, reason's analytical habit?

We may pause a long time, deciding. Perhaps for a brainy species like ours with a long, animal past still warmly alive in our bloodstream, deciding isn't yet possible.

ᦙ

Up a tight, tunnel-like passage out of Chaco Canyon I climb toward the ruin called Pueblo Alto, squeezing through sideways, my pack's nylon rubbing like static as I pass below grotesque alcoves and grottoes and then, from that umbilical crevice, emerge again into sun among flora whose colors, at the arid edge of life, manage only a starved spectrum. Ash-gray lichen. Lichen gray-brown. Lichen of yellowish green. They mottle acre-wide slabs of coyote-colored sandstone littered with crumbly detritus from strata so soft as to seem almost friable. And what isn't sandstone is sand, itself mottled or stippled by acres of sullen bitterbrush and tinder-dry sage barely knee high. Twigs of cliff rose, heavily bagwormed. Shrubs of squaw-bush, random and famished, looking like basket cases.

If some psychologist testing my word associations should read out a phrase like "the sacred," I'd not be surprised to hear myself think, "Chaco." *Aloud* I might say "a vacuum," but my thought wouldn't agree. Further associating on "sacred" in relation to Chaco Canyon's terrain, I might add "desolate, eerie, *real*." A place where stream currents are sand, where swallows soften cliff walls with mud nests by the hundreds, and where any clouds easing between you and the sun count for small mercies.

Now, revisiting Chaco, such a word cluster again *insists* on recurring. Never "beautiful," though maybe that's what Chaco can seem after a while, in an eerie, most real, and most desolate manner. Eerie because, if five-story ruins and finely finished walls mean anything, along the shallow canyon formed by the Chaco Wash there once arose an Anasazi culture so flourishing as to be—in this barren setting—well-nigh inexplicable. Called "the Chaco Phenomenon," its rise and decline created, then abandoned, the most impressive buildings in all North America. Theories abound to explain both Chaco's thriving villages and their desertion. Each plausible conjecture holds sway, then is controverted, discarded, leaving questions of use and abandonment more perplexed than before.

All of that is another story, in which "ceremonial center" is a currently fashionable hypothesis. I've spoken with one cutting-edge researcher who hopes spectrographic identification of turquoise kinds, thus of their various geographical sources, may unlock some of the mystery by revealing trade routes. For now, though, this arid region of sand and rock (whose climate wasn't much different back then) makes Chaco's many Great Houses, with their innumerable rooms and astonishing masonry walls, a Sphinx whose riddle has yet to be solved.

Yet not "ghostly," not "haunted." Not to me. Not under this sunfire that today, June 20, burns off every last romantic fume I might project onto its wind-bitten, sun-rotten landscape: Chaco's ruins are too rock ribbed and actual for misty notions. What's more, having arrived a day before the solstitial event I've come not so much to see as to feel, and be part of, I find the word "desolate" more insistent than ever: place where the only visible fauna seem thin as whiptails scuttling under low ledges, and where raven caws nag at stillness like a mate. A badlands, in fact.

Along the sunstruck trail's gradual rise, I think of the Hopi god Masau'u and his bleak invitation to "the people," who were debating whether or not to emerge from their underground world into this one. As reported by the early ethnologist-photographer H. R. Voth, Masau'u had said, "Now this is the way I am living here. I am living here in poverty. I have not anything; this is the way I am living here. Now if you are willing to live here that way too, with me and share this life, why come, you are welcome." Chaco, the Hopi mesas—his appraisal certainly fits their terrain, though the Hopi lands, more than 130 miles west, make Chaco seem verdant.

Midafternoon, walking now on sand, now on bare rock, I notice that my June 20th shadow falls almost wholly underfoot. Except for trail cairns, no human sign for miles and miles. With my pack's tiny thermometer reading 94 degrees, and the only shade the size of my straw hat, I nonetheless love exploring desert alone. The face burns like fever. Breezes are blessings. Least things seem considerable.

An honest god, Masau'u, whose bleak invitation I like having by heart. "Now this is the way I am living here . . . I have not anything." If Masau'u also had a horrible side (and he did, quite a grisly one) . . . well, that's how things are.

Sand, sage, naked stone in scorched colors. And on naked stone, where rain can linger inside micro-dunes of windblown sand, a tiny oasis may meet the eye like a gift. One such, about five feet long and four feet wide, has been colonized by tufted grasses, just a few, and by timid, trial-size versions of sagebrush. I smile at their optimism and wish them well. Over the same stretch of sandstone are glyphs written when this stratum was sea bottom: rusty, tubelike forms of fossil crustaceans whose lives were barely less simple than these scribbles they traced over slime. Our precedent. Telling something of what we were, but nothing of what we might become.

A couple of turkey vultures float toward me with that sidling motion they have, then to my left three more. Despite their taste for dead flesh, I find their slow veer and glide graceful. For several hundred yards they follow, soundlessly dipping, rising—as if assessing my immediate future. Maybe they know something? If I were Anasazi, or even Pueblo, I would *know* that they do. If I were Anasazi, I'd know this arid land to be teeming with spirits.

ᔕ

Feeling the loss of age-old deities and mythic beliefs, the German poet Schiller regretted science's "disenchantment of the world." But well over a century earlier, Galileo had mathematicized the heavens. On Earth, whereas plants and animals had once had "virtues" and "qualities" benign or malign, their semiethical natures waned to mere unmysterious fact. In science, therefore, the "value" now assigned to any cause or effect is a number. Forget "the sacred." No effect or cause has greater value, in a moral sense, than any other. Scientifically speaking, that stands to reason.

Yet if I were asked to reason forth a world devoid of sacrality I could do no better than remember one from two centuries back, as sketched by Schiller's French contemporary, the Marquis Pierre Simon de Laplace. His mathematical and astronomical studies had already led him to say that if, somehow, he could know the precise position and energy of every particle in the universe at a specific instant, he could then foresee every single event from there to the end of time. Which is to say—though he perhaps didn't need to—there's nothing in nature more divine than in any other hunk of clockwork.

An evacuated universe. My ancestral voices weaken at the prospect. "We simply can't live there," they whimper. I know. As it is, they almost don't. Besides, if wisdom works retrospectively, I'm their elder, and they my thumb-sucking children, who—logic be damned—partly begot such mind as I have. Poor blithering progenitors! I guess it's they who think Chaco sacred. Yet it's I, an ephemeral form taken by permanent atoms, who am finding this trail to a high ruin worthwhile.

ᔥ

All around the skeletal chunks of masonry walls called Pueblo Alto, sherds litter the powdery sand like stifled voices. Sherds abound, and because Chaco's complex of village-size Great Houses—the largest with more than six hundred rooms—had dwindled to complete desertion by A.D. 1300, any sherd here should be well past half a thousand years old. Pottery bits lie scattered in such atypical abundance as to imply that these ruins, when they were hale and four-square, had been a place where the gesture of vessel-breaking was once part of some ritual. Delving into trash middens here, archaeologist W. James Judge has recently estimated the number of ceramic vessels broken at Pueblo Alto to be 150,000! What meager yet rich lives did that gesture enhance? More animal bones have been found here than at other ruins, so feasting may have been part of those rites, but because I've seen not so much as a rodent all afternoon, and not many lizards—which the Anasazi never ate—orgies of meat-eating seem unlikely. Whereas potter's clay is dirt cheap.

Despite glare and hot wind I wander off-trail looking for a scrap of low-fired clay that speaks to me, one with what anthropologists call "mana"—if I believed in mana. Painted sherds allow my hand to come close to the potter's hand, probably a woman's, as with her tiny brush of chewed yucca fiber she traced a significant design. To hold some nubbin of shattered pot does seem a form of touching—and a form of piety, too, since each worthless, carefully painted oddment is a condensation of human travail and joy in patience. But I then replace each bit so carefully, so exactly, that the eventual archaeologist we're saving the past for won't be misled. Alone, unhassled, we often love more people than they or we ever know. As surely as all prayer is to the self, such trifling pieties are also—to the self in others.

Half shaded by clumped yucca basks a lizard so bedizened in his gaudy blue-green as to seem smugly vainglorious about owning a hide of live turquoise. When my slowly nearing hand gets too close for comfort, off he skitters into thicketed bitterbrush. I spit on the caked grit of two sherds he seemed to be guarding, then with my thumb rub an ancient design back into sunlight.

Both fragments show swirls on a reddish ground. They must derive from the same rather handsome pot. Another sherd reveals the same reddish slip, but on its inside surface the careful hachure of black lines implies a different hand, while its outside carries a single bold stroke in white. Another bears brownish slip, and on its inside only; but with my magnifier I see by the microscopic lichens flecking the unslipped outer surface that it must have lain here a long while indeed. Lichens of their type require many centuries to grow. The same magnifier shows the pot's inner surface lightly scored as if by actual use. Still another sherd, about the width of a tea bag, is a dim, dull gray—till I turn it over and gasp at the vivid black-on-white I recognize as classic Chacoan: fine, razor-edged brush strokes in black delineate their share of the pot's geometrical figure against a ground whose clay slip has remained surprisingly white. How fresh and companionable their yesterday seems to my hand! Time's disintegrations. My thumb, testing the fragment's roughest edge, remembers having once done so with shrapnel.

ⓢ

Pueblo Alto, like much else in Chaco, remains a conundrum. As a major terminus of Chaco's even more mysterious road system, its site high above the canyon affords a panoramic sweep of almost the entire Anasazi world. Turning from Huerfano Butte north to the Jemez Mountains east, then back to the snowy San Juans far north in Colorado, to the Chuska Mountains, far west as Arizona, and south toward Hosta Butte and Mount Taylor, I fill with hundred-mile vistas in which a desert floor's gray-greens and dapple of floating cloud shadows recede toward haze-blue remotenesses—sky-and-earth spaces so overwhelming that the actual ruins are nothing. Yet they once included Alto's two hundred rooms surrounding a plaza almost a hundred yards wide.

Given much else known about Anasazi culture, and as perhaps *the* most important hub of enigmatic roads more symbolic than practical, Pueblo Alto's site must have been "sacred." Built on a north/south alignment with the white summits of Colorado's San Juans, and thus with the great Anasazi center of Mesa Verde, with Casa Rinconada down in the canyon, and with the Tsin Kletsin Ruin across the canyon, it's a good bet that the pueblo's accurate positioning answered some requirement of sacral power.

If we can believe scholarly assessments of the sacred among so-called primitive religions worldwide—such as those in works by Emile Durkheim, Rudolf Otto, Mircea Eliade, E. R. Dodd, Roger Callois, Jean-Jacques Wunenburger, or Clifford Geertz—to cite but a few—it seems clear that Indians around here held the sacred to be just that: a power. Rituals and ceremonies were gestural alignments of one's self and community with such power; a question of *with,* not against.

For neither ancient Greeks nor modern Pueblos have relations with gods been a question of worship, in our sense, nor of love. No Greek ever said, "I love my Zeus," though every believing Greek feared his power. The sacred, understood as Indians have understood it, is no more "good" or "bad" than, to cite physical analogies, lightning or gravity. To the Anasazi, especially in places like Chaco, orienting one's life and group with relation to the sacred as often and in as many modes as possible was, if historically based inference means anything, never a question of being "religious" as we understand the term. More a question of *Being*. And of survival.

On my trek down from Pueblo Alto's panoramas back into the canyon, I see what looks like broken pottery everywhere, but know mostly it isn't; just rock chips, many of them "slipped" with caliche, a calcium carbonate often found in sandstone. Among sherds I had picked up and put back were one or two I wanted to pocket, but my archaeological conscience forbade it—as do the stiff penalties protecting these sites. More immediate, though, than science or fines was my wanting not to be wrongly aligned. Keeping even one sherd would have ever-so-slightly skewed my stance at tomorrow's sunrise.

"Now this is the way I am living here," Masau'u reminds me. "I am living here in poverty. I have not anything; this is the way I am living here."

§

A pleasant habit of late-afternoon campgrounds is how voices lower as the sun does, as if to blend with the evening. Our sites along the canyon's humongous cliff fractures come under the spell of its muted, sundown color. Ruddying light softens boxcar chunks till the palomino rock glows like chalks in a set of pastels. Or like harmonious earth hues in a Navajo weaving.

Where somebody spilled a lot of water, hundreds of cliff swallows take turns sipping from its turbid puddle. Late evening sun comes through their backlit wings, which they don't fold but keep nervously widespread and fluttering, never settling completely but drinking tiptoe, as if afraid to leave flight entirely. As if they love this sky more than anything.

The family camped on my left seem desert-ready. Their clunky van has a microkitchen, bunks for their two teenage girls, roll-up awning along one side, luggage carrier loaded with gear and folding chairs—the works. He's a well-muscled, dark-bearded forty or so. While the honey-blonde woman stirs pasta sauce, I jokingly ask him if they've toured Zimbabwe in that van. He grins.

"Only had it two months," he says, "which is how long we've been married. Second time around for each of us."

Chaco being reachable only after thirty miles of dirt ruts and washboarded gravel, nobody visits in passing. So I ask, "What's it about Anasazi ruins that interests you? What's the attraction?"

"Human continuity," he says without a moment's delay. "Human intelligence."

An answer so terse startles me. Most people I question grope for words they never quite find. Besides, they're often slow to open up for a stranger.

In another part of the campground, though, while cliff swallows fly headlong into stone, then out again, a woman named Soledad doesn't skimp on self-revelation. "I'm leaving Sedona," she says. "It's spoiled. They've put in a Safeway, and condos. Houses going up all over the place. Californians moving in. A hundred dollars for a reading, for *one* reading. Just an ordinary 'You're going to find this wonderful man and go off into the sunset with him.' A hundred dollars for that!" In derision she tosses her mane of long, long hair, a dark and coppery red. Her face, plucked eyebrows, and puffy figure are those of an indoor woman well into her forties. Chaco seems an unlikely stop.

"Oh, I've done everything," she continues. "Sold precision instruments to the military. I've run a school, I've done massage. I'm heading up to Durango, to scope it out, see if I want to live there. I do channeling. People I work with, I've been using visualizing a lot lately. I get them to visualize, see who they are that way. Also I use hypnotism. Two months ago I had an experience. It changed my life. It was so unusual, if you told people about it, they'd say you were crazy."

"Did it involve a UFO?" I guess aloud, and regret it.

She gives me a look and chokes up, her face distorting as she starts to weep, then recovers, goes on. "People don't understand how important their own individual lives are. Our lives are very big. Each person is huge. You have no idea. I look at that raven swooping over and try to understand what he's telling me. Each thing here is telling us something. These canyon walls are telling us something right now. This place has something to say to us. That's why I came. I need to find out who I am. Who I really am. It's why I changed my name to Soledad."

I told her about my acquaintance Margie. "Somehow she wants to live like a river, so she changed her name to Rio. Just Rio, period."

"Yes," she nods. "There's a lot of that in Sedona. I met a woman who when I asked what her name was said, 'Deborah You-Name-It.' That was her name: You-Name-It. And Greg Powerlines. That's what he changed to. Some of those names you wouldn't believe. There's this book, *The Mayan Factor* by Jose Arguelles. It discusses the dates of galactic windows. Certain times when those windows are open and we can receive significant experiences. Two months ago I had an experience you wouldn't believe. It showed me I didn't know. I thought I knew, but I didn't really know. Now I'm trying to find out. I'll stay till June 23rd. That's a significant date for me. Something significant is going to happen."

⑤

Ravens or canyon walls telling us things isn't a New Age notion by any means. Animism, the feeling that all nature—cloud, tree, boulder—is enspirited, alive, may be the oldest form of belief. Anasazi descendants, the Pueblos, have long lived in a world where a raven, for example, is a plain raven and a stone an ordinary old stone; yet that raven or stone may simultaneously be something else, a manifestation of the sacred. Pueblo beliefs, however, exist within a worldview far more complex than animism. As to that, whether we espouse complex beliefs or none at all, the most intellectual among us can revert to animism instantly. Everyone does. We turn proto-primitive when, for example, barking our shins on a chair, we angrily "punish" it with a kick whose impulse is ten thousand times older than we are.

§

Unrumpling from a sleeping bag into early chill at 4:15 A.M., I'm a bit surprised by how many others are already stirring: we communal strangers, whom the forthcoming sunrise has drawn to this patch of New Mexican sand. From a table nearby, a gas stove begins its low roar. A pot lid clatters. The bearded owner of the van uses hushed tones and few words while his adolescent girls, still horizontal, catch a few extra winks. Wanting to arrive at Casa Rinconada well ahead of dawn, I postpone coffee and climb into my white pickup, sorry the gravel crackles so loudly as I ease northward out of the campground.

In summer desert, morning and evening are matched enchantments. Mornings, before the sun warms to its work, you can still breathe easy. You inhale early air like a fragrance, because that's what it is. Evenings, the moment sun dips from sight, you exhale as if shucking off a pack carried all day. That's why, parked and approaching Chaco's greatest kiva on foot, I find it almost natural at this best of hours to hear flute music floating, so it seems, out of canyon stone just back of the site.

Though a misnomer, Casa Rinconada names the canyon's most unusual Great Kiva—"great" in Chacoan archaeology meaning "big." Whereas most kivas occur within village walls, this one differs conspicuously by being set off and apart, on a knoll scruffy with rabbit brush and thistle. The kiva forms the usual circle but is an unusual sixty-three feet wide. Moreover, its walls stand twelve to sixteen feet high, with such careful symmetries built into their features that to sketch and discuss the implications would require a monograph. Irregular locations, among an otherwise symmetrically regular row of niches all round the inner wall, would need a chapter alone. The kiva's careful orientation to astronomical north and the cardinal directions, with each of four huge roof supports placed accurately at the intercardinals, can't be other than deliberate, not to mention symmetries of doors and floor plan. After studying these and much else with transit and steel tape, archaeoastronomer Ray Williamson has declared Casa Rinconada unique: nothing like it in the entire Southwest.

In the rose glow before dawn, people already line the kiva's outer rim of masonry, dozens of people, with more trickling up the gravel path toward it. On my right, one gray-bearded man, perfectly bald, adjusts his JVC camcorder on its tripod. I look down into a now roofless space where for generations Anasazi ceremonies kept Chaco's communities properly aligned with the sacred. Within it I count another thirty-three people. Apart from our jackets and sweaters and hugging ourselves in the chilly air, curiosity, cameras, and shorts are what most of us have in common—all but the ranger in his long pants of forest green. And a few Indians, whose covered legs remind me how rarely the reservation Indians wear shorts, much less tote cameras, except in ritual clowning that parodies Anglos like us.

As with everything else about Chaco, this solstitial event raises questions. Archaeological restoration of the kiva left it roofless but did rehabilitate its circular shape with the twenty-eight niches evenly sized and spaced all round its wall of laid stone. Six additional niches, different in size and placement, complicate our conjectures. We've gathered to see a ray of the newly risen sun pass through one window and hit a special niche, though what that might've meant to the Anasazi nobody can say.

6:05 A.M. Fifteen minutes to go. I use a few of them to sound out the presiding ranger, a tall, robust, and white-bearded man who, however improbably, claims his name really is Cornucopia. At last night's campfire talk it grew clear he's well-versed in archaeoastronomy. Instead of nursing our potential credulity, he sketches the facts.

"Photos taken during restoration show sections of wall entirely collapsed. I mean, entirely. In fact, the kiva is 70 to 75 percent restored. Then there's a problem with that northeast window, the one the beam of sunlight comes through. It may not have been part of the original building. I mean, presuming the restoration guys got it right, did they get it in the right spot? Where the Anasazi builders first put it, if they did?"

Ranger Cornucopia's informative tone draws bystanders. Soon he's surrounded. "Archaeologists doing the work couldn't foresee what questions might come up fifty years later. Besides, restoration crews back then weren't always careful to nail down everything in their documentation. And what about roof lines? The kiva's roof had to be massive, that we know, but how far did it overhang? Would it have been in the way?"

He shrugs, indicating that none of these questions is answerable. But there's more, and for true believers, perhaps worse yet: a final impediment not at all doubtful.

Cornucopia broaches it tactfully, not wanting to trample on anybody's sensibilities; but neither does his scientific bent incline him to pussyfoot. His height, white beard, broad-brimmed hat, and ranger uniform lend authority as he says, "We know the wooden pillars supporting this kiva's roof were between twenty-four and twenty-six inches wide." We wonder what those timbers have to do with anything. He then adds, "But we also know exactly where each pillar stood, and know one of them would have partly blocked off that particular shaft of sunlight."

Archaeoastronomy aside, those huge timbers are a story in themselves. Though lacking draft animals and any sort of wheel, builders in Chaco somehow brought whole forests into this canyon where (with *possibly* a few rare exceptions) no trees higher than bushes existed. At a conservative estimate, five thousand trees went into the building of Chetro Ketl alone—not the largest of Chaco's Great Houses. As the canyon's use of traves and beams grew, numerous logs big as Rinconada's roof timbers were conveyed from as far as sixty miles distant, on labor that must have been driven by sacral motives of some sort.

Many of us who had long known of that prodigious log hauling hadn't thought about roof supports blocking solar rays. Oh, we knew that certain doubts had arisen, yet here we are, expectant —almost reverently so. Why?

For one thing, we know Anasazi builders were capable of accurately aligning this kiva, as align it they did, on true, astronomical north and the cardinal directions. Hand compasses aren't transits; still, my own compass, magnetic declination duly allowed for, has roughly corroborated that alignment here, at structures across the canyon, and at sites a hundred miles from Chaco. We know, too, that the famous "sun dagger" high on Fajada Butte here in the canyon creates clever solstitial effects undoubtedly planned for. But why, I ask myself, should we have gathered to witness a calendrical orientation so dubiously prehistoric? For that matter, why is the fellow right below me inside the kiva fingering prayer beads with his right hand? Despite my years of going out to meet dawn, I'm finding this group of ours fascinating as the solstice itself.

Nominal sunrise already happened at 5:52 A.M., but the light we're anticipating won't clear the near buttes till about 6:23, still nine minutes away. Clustered with others at the kiva's outer rim stands Soledad, she of the coppery hair. What's she thinking, I wonder. Or visualizing?

Earlier, people had been darting anxious glances eastward toward a reef of low cloud that might have prevented direct sun from entering the kiva. But now a spot of sunlight the size of a child's torso appears within it, twelve feet northwest of the special niche and well above. Across the canyon, excavation of a Great Kiva nearly this large showed similar niches to contain ritual apparatus, beads, necklaces of remarkable craftsmanship and length, as well as lumps of turquoise. Sacral offerings? Amulets? Among historic Pueblos, turquoise has long been a sun stone.

Seven minutes to go. While the spot of sunlight moves like an actor coming on stage in a solemn drama, down inside Casa Rinconada quite apart from the others sits a beautiful, dark-haired young woman in full lotus posture, facing that beam with closed lids. Across her back is slung a flute case of gray buckskin. The cosmetic blush on her cheeks surprises me. Never till now have I seen anyone wear makeup in the desert.

6:17 A.M. Six minutes left. Above that young woman and around the west wall, whose upper stones brighten from dawn's rust red to golden, the sun has projected our shadows like a frieze or painting *inside* the kiva. Because actual and absent shadows weigh equally, we see by those shadows that our lives might be anyone's; might be Anasazi or Greek, Celt or Briton, watching the seasons trade places. As that solar ray inches closer to *the* niche, we become blood cousins of shadows long disembodied.

Finally it's there: a rectangle of sunlight not quite congruent with its boxlike recess of stone, but about the same width, as if both recess and aperture had been made for each other, and thus almost a fit, near enough for releasing mixed murmurs of exclamation, analysis.

ᔕ

"To be Anasazi," I used to speculate, ". . . but how?" In one way, of course, we can't. But why bother trying, since we already *are* Anasazi in another very natural way: that of the seasons, their progression, the year cycle. Like temples the world over, the great kivas at Chaco were laid out and built to align with the cosmos literally and symbolically. Not only were north, south, east, and west accurately reflected in Casa Rinconada's main parts; so were northeast, southeast, southwest, and northwest. Additionally, the vertical axis of *Homo erectus* (thus of *Homo sapiens* and all humankind) was reflected by an actual hole in the roof and a symbolic hole in the floor: so to north, south, east, and west were added two directions more: up and down. Those are the crucial six directions of Pueblos even today. Moreover, the kiva's circular walls were part below ground, part above, reflecting our past and our present: up from earth into this sunlit air. All in all, a Great Kiva's stone, adobe, and timber took the shape of both the cosmos and every human destiny.

It still does. That's what temples offer: a place for knowing what we are, and what this world is. Or should I say "where"? Same thing. Any sacred building's layout and symbols offer alignment, orientation. They give directions without saying a word.

So does the sun. To the Anasazi, it gave the six directions that continue to center Pueblo religions, making the shape of the world the shape of a year.

By fifth grade most children can diagram Earth's orbit and may even know exactly how far our planet is tilted: 23.5 degrees. Until going out to see for myself, however, my sense of all that had come mainly from books. Then, because living at the foot of a mesa made it easy, I began watching, dawn by dawn, the sun's yearly trip from south to north, and back again. Only in seeing how astonishingly *far* that is on a real horizon did I take sun travel into my blood and bones. To a friend you can explain, "The total swing is twice Earth's tilt: 47 degrees." Whereupon that friend will nod assent, but won't get it.

Not really. Not unless he stands high enough, daily enough, to see thereby a living, years-familiar horizon replace mere concept. If he follows the sun's north/south travel over actual earth, he then may say, as I have, "My God, what a span! Enormous!"

Later, if he's like me, he'll appreciate how *immediate* the six directions are to Pueblos who still farm in the sunbelt, as their Anasazi forebears did for thousands of years. Daily, the sun's rise and set teach four of the six: up and down, east and west. Its annual journey from south to north teaches the remaining two. Small wonder, then, that Indians growing the so-called sacred triad of corn, beans, and squash built solar alignment into dwellings and kivas, into rituals, music, fabrics, pots, masks, body paint, and therefore into every blessed day. In the high Southwest, farming at over six thousand feet, you deal with a short growing season. Knowing *when* to sow is crucial. And when you reap, it's like harvesting prayers.

For us, technology has so mediated nature that we may pass days and weeks unmindful of solar paths, even as our days flow away within them. So long as we remain unmindful, however, those prehistoric peoples without writing or metal will still have known more than we do. But when our lives grow fully aware of their open and close under an up-and-down sun; when that sun's resurrection in us becomes the news we prefer to be reading; when its rise is our best recurrence but never a habit—then in that, if in nothing else, we're kin to those who built Rinconada.

§

He reminds me of Kokopelli, the hunchbacked flute player I've often seen in petroglyphs near Anasazi sites. Voluble, lively, visiting with everybody in the campground, wearing shorts but no shirt, he stands 5'4" in sandals, his toes *very* tan, his shins freckled with the scabs of old bites. Gray hair to his bare shoulders, a large sunburnt nose over his grizzled beard, he carries his wooden flute in a buckskin case slung at his back, explaining, "I play it for therapy."

"Why not for music?" I ask.

He grins as if that made him mine for a while. "I'm on sabbatical," he says. "From the psychology department at Elmira, New York. I teach family psychology, but this is my leave time, so I'm camping cross-country. My ex and our two sons are back East. Spent a month at Sedona before coming here. Sure, I showed up at Casa Rinconada for dawn, why not? Who knows, there might be some sort of presence. I might be touched by something of that. Yesterday evening I sat in one of the rooms in that biggest ruin, Pueblo Bonito, and played my flute, same reason. Maybe after all those centuries of habitation in this canyon—over two thousand years of it—well, maybe something's there. Maybe I can be part of that, but if not, it's still a great place. At Sedona there's this rock—'the Cathedral' they call it—but it's bigger than any cathedral. I've seen it glow more than once. Not a lighting effect. Instead there's this *glow*. I hadn't been drinking, hadn't been doing drugs, and others who were with me saw it too. What the explanation is, I don't know, but I did see it—the whole formation glowed. Sedona people talk about a geological intrusion causing it. From here I'm heading up to Taos, but," he says, spreading his arms as if to sweep the canyon into them, "definitely, I'm coming back to Chaco."

After returning to my tent site, I pump my aging Coleman stove and set about brewing coffee. Campground ravens had started in hours ago, cawing and yakking, tossing themselves from rimrock for low swoops over sandy canyon floor. By 8 A.M. bees are already swarming among tiny yellow florets topping a big clump of prince's plume, so iced tea, if I had any ice, would make far better sense; but morning rites can be cosmic or trivial, and hot caffeine is one of mine. Waiting for it to perk, I replay what my Kokopelli had said. He had couched his openness to a spiritual "something" in terms of "maybe" and "might" and "if" and "if not, okay." Had spoken of a presence that could touch him, possibly. Or possibly not. Sedona, Chaco, Taos—less a vision quest than a vision question? Too vague for the sacred, yet open to "something."

He's far from unique in that. As our dawn gathering melted away in twos and threes from Casa Rinconada, my Kokopelli's tentative style had been the norm. People knew the "calendrical effect" may not have been there for the Anasazi, but knew the kiva's symbolic structure certainly was. And knew if that effect were entirely wishful on our part, our wish to gather at Chaco's most significant kiva wasn't. It was as real as the relation between dawn, there, and ourselves; between ourselves and the sun's six directions.

⑤

Most kivas are circular, as are many temples (our very word for which is related to *tempus,* Latin for time). Aligned with the sunyear, Casa Rinconada's circular walls had centered this morning for us by being, as it had been for its builders, a temple built not "in the middle of nowhere" but at the world's center. Its stones still believe time is a circle. Like many a ceremonial kiva in active use by Pueblos, it's a temple where time comes round.

Whether or not we Anglos consider a site like Casa Rinconada sacred or merely interesting, Pueblos respect it enough to resent encroachments that have grown increasingly common. "Oh yes," says Ranger Susan Digrazio, the crown of whose Smokey Bear hat would barely reach Ranger Cornucopia's badge, "People come, do things, leave 'offerings'—which of course the Park Service removes."

"They 'do things'?" I ask. "Like what? What kind of things?"

"Oh, they hold ceremonies, do dances. They play flutes, finger drums. They light candles and have vigils. Not any more . . . but they did. There were lots of protests from Pueblos, who say, 'These ruins were built by our ancestors. People should respect them. Your ceremonies aren't Indian ceremonies. We don't take our drums into your churches and hold our dances.' Now the Park Service has a Pueblo advisory council to help us deal with all that."

I tell her I've seen encroachment at the Stone Lions shrine on the Pajarito Plateau of New Mexico, also an Anasazi site. It had grown so encumbered with deer-antler "offerings," baubles, and oddments that Indians finally cleared it all off. Respectful visits are one thing; spiritual trespass, quite another. Or, as a friend of mine puts it, "Some people don't have no manners."

☙

That a great many people do seem to be looking for "something" doesn't alter the fact that any "something" so wishfully, wistfully, harmlessly vague has little to do with Indian ideas of the sacred—not if that word's ancient history means anything. Nor does Christian usage count, because Christian tradition omits an ambiguity that energizes sacred power among countless unbiblical religions. In Latin, *sacer* could mean "blessed" or "cursed," reflecting a typically ambiguous penetration of opposites. In contrast, scriptural religions tend literally to go by the book, and thus to codify and dogmatize what unwritten religions leave open. Christianity, especially, identifies the sacred with "good," whereas ancient Greeks and Pueblos—to cite parallel extremes—conceived the sacred in ways making "good" irrelevant, even absurd.

Since the expansion of science, earth gods and sky gods have faced loss of habitat; however, in the wake of Romanticism, ongoing attempts by Americans to relocate (with Thoreau) "salvation" in wilderness, and to relocate the sacred in nature, may imply similarly diminished ideas about what their praise or cheerleading aims to exalt. Wilderness having become an artifact of legislatures, its sacral promise often gets commodified into recreation. No more relevantly than the Greek god Apollo or the Hopi god Masau'u can nature be called "good." Nature *is.* And, like the traditional sacred, is a power inescapable. By projecting a secularized sacrality onto nature as a sort of benign whiff exuded from forests, vernal woods, or whitewater streams, we may forget that sacred power is traditionally grounded in the supernatural, whereas, and by definition, nature is natural. Yet a Hopi leader could say, "The Hopi land *is* the Hopi religion," because to Pueblos nature is never only natural.

§

At 5:30 P.M. under an overcast sky creating a mood wholly unlike the blue skies of early morning, I find myself well above the canyon, miles from Casa Rinconada. After having legged it up trail to a pictograph much discussed by archaeoastronomers, I've come even farther up to visit the big unexcavated ruin called Peñasco Blanco. Now, sitting by its massive rudiments of broken perfection, beneath a sky gray as tin, alone for hours with just ravens or turkey vultures, though few even of those, I stare out across leagues of what looks more than ever like a featureless steppe. Back along miles of trail, nobody coming; nobody here, nothing human in sight. All around this ruin and beyond, not a tree. Nor many bushes; none higher than a couple of feet, and few even that tall. Otherwise, vegetation is gray-green tufts of whiskery grass. Way off to the southeast stretch the sands of Chaco Wash; dry, bone white, and broad. Seventy yards off, a coyote who long ago chose dust for his colors goes nosing in and out of low sage. I ask myself, "How can even he make a living here?" Yet somehow he gets by.

All the same, though "bleak" should name my mood, it doesn't. "Emptiness," yes, and one I'm well content to sit quietly filled with. Its slight sadness feels like wisdom, as if that's what I, too, had come to Chaco for.

As I scan that meager terrain, an awareness I'd dismissed yesterday up at Pueblo Alto recurs: "This is the face of the sacred." Immediately I'm puzzled. Yesterday I had shrugged, "You're just saying that." And maybe I had been. But its return, so unbidden, so odd . . . again sets me wondering. Why does so quirky a thought feel true?

Maybe it's because, when you sit for a couple of hours amid the ruins of the human, looking out over gritty miles of stunted sage and rabbit brush and yucca, what you see does the talking. "The gods do not love anyone," it seems to say. "The gods do not hate anyone." Then, too, Peñasco Blanco's long-abandoned rooms, in such a landscape, seem to explain the gods' difficult existence, whose pathos looks like a version of our own: the human condition. Even the rain-famished bitterbrush, yucca, the writhing sage say the same. Their stunted growth is pathetic, heroic.

Surely that's what the Hopi god Masau'u was saying: "Now this is the way I am living here. I am living here in poverty. I have not anything. . . ."

᭤

No lands feel more desolate than those of the Hopi, no religion more beautiful or complex. That very desolation must have begotten such beauty and complexity. Encircled by utter indifference in every empty direction, you could feel yourself the least of beings, the merest speck; or you could sense yourself as the focus of spirits and sacred powers—without ceasing, however, to realize that in such vastitudes everyone's daily affairs hither and yon around your tiny pueblo count for no more than the trickles of ant people busily seething round *their* anthill. So you'd work up all the self-importance you could muster. You'd need painted ceremonies, masks, rituals—merely to keep on striving. A lot of just such gaudily painted apparatus was excavated from the Great Kiva at Chetro Ketl. Maybe the Bluebird chief Hermequaftewa spoke truer than he knew in declaring that the Hopi land and Hopi religion are one.

From Peñasco Blanco my last mile or so runs along the foot of cliffs whose angle to lowering sun makes the hundreds of petroglyphs easier to spot. I've already threaded in and out among greasewood clumps and snakeweed, prospecting these same mocha walls for rock art and photographing dozens of glyphs, so by now

I'm more foot-weary than curious. But symbols pecked into stone that long ago are addictive. It's impossible *not* to keep an eye out for ones overlooked earlier. Even more impossible not to feel a surge of anger at realizing, again, that well over half of those prehistoric designs have been vandalized: names or initials scratched over ancient spirals, animal forms hacked into, Anasazi motifs crudely faked, stupid doodles. From the ancient hands of Peñasco Blanco I've descended to hands amused by defacing their own past. We'll never reach it, I guess, but those obliterations imply that our greatest wisdom might be in living gently enough to make others wise.

Unwilling to let bad vibes be this evening's last word, farther down-trail I take the risk of climbing well above vandal height for a look at figures I'd spotted earlier but couldn't make out. Only half visible in the deep shade of an overhang, their pink understone just barely lighter than the slightly darker surface rock, five stick-figure people stand facing me. Because they vary from six to eight inches tall, I imagine them a family with animals, rich in little more than the ceremony of life. Above, to their right, are pecked outlines of three desert bighorns in profile. The overhang has kept them unweathered, fresh as yesterday morning. They don't say who left them or why. They simply *are*. "Me too," I think, "for now, at least." Then, wary of loose rock and rattlers, I climb carefully down.

⑤

Traveling alone as I do, I let my campground suppers take shortcuts. Especially when wind-withered and grit-bitten and baked, I find that cooking messes up pots and spoons that'll need cleaning just when the evening sky usually prefers my full attention. After Peñasco Blanco, what's quickest turns out to be the whole wheat of naked bagels and warm beer.

A wise choice. For tonight's show the huge thunderhead southwest of us keeps illuminating its billows from inside, and the flare-ups of lightning seem all the more eerie by their scarcely audible thunder. North of all that, veils and tatters of ghost rain pour their slow-motion downfalls toward Earth while saturating themselves in color from a sun already down: now vivid Niagaras of orange, now scarlet, now modulating to wide sashes of magenta, then to the dimmest tinge of burgundy going purple. Ghost rain, because not a drop of it hits the ground. So in my camp chair I munch and sip and let those downfalls reveal warps in the faraway atmosphere; yet I know the beauty in air's grand powers depends on that distance. Meanwhile, sundown's last afterglow on canyon stone makes fractured walls creaturely, steeps them in tints so brief as to have lives of their own.

To be Anasazi . . . I'd need to feel the thunderhead's internal flashes as in some way deific, but I can't. Friction of atoms in vapor, electron differential, voltage: discharge. Must we lie about such things? Like the nonexistent gods, mystery abounds and is endless. Yet if I replace "mystery" with "mechanism," I'm back to the Marquis de Laplace and a cosmos that works like a gearbox. Why should that beget an unmetaphysical shudder? Why this need for our daily fix of transcendence?

Twilight having given birth to the evening's first stars, I feel the fast chilldown of Chaco Canyon's six-thousand-foot altitude. A pile jacket's my answer, while a foam pad on the chair insulates my backside. Body warmth thus cozied, I enjoy night's nippy air on windburnt face and hands. Ravens all roosting somewhere? Apparently so. Cliff swallows gone, too.

All across our small campground it's again sweater time; hour of campfire murmurs, splash of tossed dishwater; hour of flashlights floating hip-high toward or from the latrine, of voices calling to know what somebody's done with the matches; but above all, literally, hour of New Mexican stars. Anasazi stars, too, if we could see with eyes made of dust. Unsmothered by town glow or smog, the clear dark sizzles with their particulate fire. Lots of antique gods and goddesses up there. What all didn't our ancestors see in the stars! For us, it's the hour of constellations looked up to. Hour of the Milky Way, its wildly fathomless, overarching sweep. Hour of thinking, "our galaxy," then beyond. Hour of irises widened for that neighbor galaxy, the one in the Andromeda constellation, whose light—just now arriving—first set out long before any reasoning eye had yet evolved to see it. Hour therefore of the entirely human.

That we've all of us freely chosen to show up at Chaco—does that imply some tinge of preference for living in a mystery, not a mechanism? Tonight, as my eyes find it impossible not to see invisible lines between stars, I'm aware that terms like "the Cosmos," "the Universe," "the All"—thin as they are—imply a sort of transcendent beyond, a dimension we lean toward without ever being there: the sacred place, Blessed Isles, Elysian Fields. One minor proof that our humanity is created by language might be just that ease with which our minds set out for some near-metaphysical or sacramental *elsewhere* in words.

To have been accultured by one's mother tongue and people doesn't feel humiliating. I've nothing inside me that this world and others haven't put there. Tongues living and dead have induced me to feel I might loiter within the neighborhood of "the sacred," as I've done here in Chaco, even while realizing that the term names little more than an attitude: a mental event certain places may conduce to. But the sacred isn't that place. A spark, a particle. A seed sown in us by humanity's long conversation with its best self. As such, is the sacred really self-love echoed back to sound like a call? A circular transaction? For me, its "place" exists anytime we stand at a center, the center of a moment: our own widest awareness of, and agreement to be, who and where we are.

Except for a not-so-slight problem. Because context alters content, that "who" depends on "where." And since "where" depends on the "who" doing the conceiving, they depend on each other. Leaving us once more with mysteries made of our ignorance. So why be surprised? Haven't the gods always been made of our own limitations? No god has qualities a human wouldn't find useful.

The greatest nature poet of ancient Rome, Lucretius, wrote to persuade the fearful, superstitious Romans of what he felt was good news: that nature is as mechanical as atoms—atoms, which the gods neither created, inhabit, nor take any interest in. Repeating his Greek idol Democritus, he reassured his contemporaries with what must have seemed cold comfort: "Nothing exists but atoms and empty space. Everything else is opinion." Oh, it's true that the tone of Lucretius's every page is haunted by the very deities his rational materialism intended to paint out of the picture; however, his great poem, "On the Nature of the Universe," honestly meant to dispel shadows that keep ghost-ridden humans from seeing where and what they truly are: surrounded by natural marvels.

For most of humankind, wonders merely natural aren't quite enough—as if our species sorely needs religious emotion to restore what analytical reason makes away with. The physicist Steven Weinberg implied as much in noting, a bit glumly, "The more the universe seems comprehensible, the more it seems pointless." So is some ever-changing "vital lie" the survival secret of our species? Without illusion would our *elan vital* expire? In short, is some form of belief, disguised or overt, our rational nature's defense against itself?

ⓢ

From the far end of the campground set apart for large groups, someone begins strumming basic chords on a guitar. Voices pick up the song, but keep it low; now clear, now faint, as night breeze rises or falls. I catch notes, a few phrases, but not the tune. Ironically, it's probably the Baptist youth group I saw pitching three large tents earlier. For them the wilderness of New Mexican stars in all their scatter and gather must truly seem heavenly. For me their brilliance is the natural dazzle of nuclear reactors spewing horrendously inconceivable energies. Manic fuel dumps in the sky—which, in theory, they are. Perhaps it's as well neither I nor any but an astrophysicist can see them only like that. Even the faintest stars give off a come-hither wink, and the brightest ones flare with radiant emotions that want to be truths.

The singing, the guitarist's amateur strums, bring to mind my flute-playing, grizzle-bearded, sandal-wearing Kokopelli on his cross-country sabbatical. Despite that glow at Sedona, surely he would have agreed that this canyon isn't in any orthodox sense "sacred." So why had he said, "Definitely, I'm coming back to Chaco"?

Is he, really? Am I? Having visited all the ruins at one time or another, I doubt it. Why should I? What reason? True, I hadn't much of a reason for coming this time, but that didn't stop me. There are places you go, simply to be there. In the old days, such going toward was called pilgrimage. Admittedly, my coming here many years in a row—driving the 450 miles from Boulder, always in time for the summer solstice—might seem pilgrimage-like. But pilgrims are credulous, whereas I'm the opposite.

From now on, recalling Chaco, I'll simply remember this morning as special, remember standing with a hundred curious others as we all watched a splash of sunlight floating slowly as time across adobe-mortared stones. Like watching the enactment of a prophecy dramatized: the sun keeping its promise.

Whether Anasazi hands had intended that particular effect or not, we had nonetheless felt its significance, had felt the kiva become a focus where our human and natural worlds, times past and time present, momentarily came together in us. We may even have realized then how near we were to our primitive souls. Not as if in some transcendent instant time's annihilations had gone into reverse, with the canyon's great houses, their backs to the wall, suddenly healing like a shattered pot, its pieces resurrecting themselves from sand and flying perfectly back into each other. Yet, however briefly, that moment really did feel like something broken made whole.

True, dawn's best insights quickly fade to mere habit, but they also recur. After all, the sun is a circle. So by next June, who knows, I might be loading my pickup, remembering, too, how morning's up-and-down sun projected our shadows onto the kiva wall where each stone knew its place—as did stones of every rubbled wall in this canyon. Like the people who put them there.

Just as we living ones need the dead to remember us and help us with our lives, the gods rely on us mortals to sustain them. In any case, at Casa Rinconada, perhaps because surrounded by the canyon's tumbledown ruination, we had felt ourselves keenly, exactly *there,* where the sun and planet were one, and were ours. Ours not to exploit but to get properly aligned with. At any rate, that's how I felt, and feeling so, thought yet again of Masau'u, rarest of deities, an honest god: "Now if you are willing to live here that way too, with me and share this life, why come, you are welcome."

Egypt, Arizona

The Anasazi girl looks up from her grinding stone and stares off, in that manner we humans have. As if seeing . . . what? Far as her own prospects? How her daughters, if any, will kneel there in turn? Just as her mother, grandmother, all women kinfolk long before them had knelt, grinding corn. Woman's work it is, among her people, and maybe all, and is most certainly work.

I've tried it. What surprise! Finding the dried corn tough as pebbles, I had to lean heavily forward on the upper stone, the *mano*, while with a steady scrubbing motion I grated away at each handful of kernels, rubbing the *mano* to and fro over a nether stone, the *metate*. After some vigorous minutes I had ground less than a quarter-cupful of meal, enough for a frito chip. Resting my back and knees, I sat a while on my haunches and pondered the lot of Indian women with a whole family of mouths to grind for. "Forget it," I thought. "Two adults, a child or so. That would take *hours*." Every day, and the day after that.

It did. In fact, Hopi oral tradition includes a story in which Hopi males take over women's work and make the same discovery in almost my words: "Hey, this corn grinding's *hard*."

So the Anasazi girl kneels, staring off inwardly. Nude but not naked, her body is lean as twelve or thirteen; yet her face isn't quite that of a child. Hair held out of the eyes by a braided headband maybe one finger wide, her daydreamy gaze sees something. Though pretty, she is also interesting. With darkly expressive eyebrows, that black hair just touching hunched shoulders. But it's her gaze that arrests me. Plus her youth, coupled to such daily drudgery like a premature fate. The mouth and eyes convey a faintest tinge of sadness. Especially the eyes. They speak of things hoped for, but which may never happen.

There's a moment in a young person's life when she sees herself—for the first time—as just anyone. The girl's expression suggests she has entered such a moment, foreseeing what's ahead: live play work die. Love, too, of course; so I'd prefer, when the moment passes, that her inner eye come to rest on a certain young male of her village, wondering how hopeful she dare become.

She is and is not Anasazi. In substance, less than ten inches long; a mere statuette, an ancient Egyptian figurine noticed years ago at the Museo Archeologico in Florence, Italy, where I liked her the oldest way: the way a young man likes the look of a particular young woman. Home I brought the memory of her on a postcard. "Sixth Dynasty" had said the display-case inscription, which puts her youth at 2300 B.C. or thereabouts. Back in my student days, culture-vulturing through Europe, I hadn't yet heard of the Anasazi, and if I had, wouldn't have given them ten seconds thought. My idea of the past was Europe. Lately, rummaging for stuff to chuck out of closets, I again came across that postcard, a plain black-and-white 3x5, amid a shoebox crammed solid with cards of paintings, basilicas, statues. They meant a lot to me then. Or so I supposed.

Now better aware who we both are, and what this world is, I value the Egyptian girl's rediscovered image over the whole boxful of others. It alone really speaks to me.

By now, too, having examined Anasazi sites across the American Southwest, having myself grown pensive over I know not how many dozens and dozens of grinding bins, having seen countless *mano* stones at rest upon their well-worn *metates,* I'm able to see how a girl of ancient Egypt is—by a visually remarkable coincidence— also classic Anasazi.

Goddess and life-giver (and worker, of course) and therefore all women. But at the same time, more: anyone young or old, homely or comely, who looks up from back-bending labor and stares day-dreamily off into somewhere. Hence Arizona in Egypt, Egypt in Arizona: one "clay statuette, many-colored," as the postcard's inscription says. Also one girl. Nobody knows who made her into it, or why. Nor can anyone ever know who on Earth such a girl may have been. On reflection, though, maybe we all do.

The Real Surreal

HORSESHOE CANYON

For years I'd been hoping one day to lay eyes on certain ancient, blood-red silhouettes that even in bad photos look ghostly. Or as a friend had put it, "real surreal." For years I'd intended to go see for myself, no idea why.

As to not knowing why, for how much of our lives have we known what we were doing? Truly *known*? Mostly, I've never. Though I've lived a long time in Colorado, I was born in the state of bemusement. At birth, no silver spoon; only a question mark. Example: why drive nearly four hundred miles (the last thirty, red dirt) just to see pictographs?

Seated this Utah evening on the rim, and I do mean the very leg-dangling *edge,* of Horseshoe Canyon, I wonder other things, too; such as, "Didn't sundown come kind of early?" But then a last roseate flood of direct rays breaks through cloud, and the wind-sculpted sandstone forms blush crimson. Gorgeous. About that I've no doubt whatever.

About the pictographs themselves I'm less sure. A man I like had said, "Oh yeah, Horseshoe Canyon. Y' gotta see 'em." But why trust his judgment four hundred miles worth? Because I love Utah canyons? Because I rather enjoy never quite knowing?

I drink beer, munch pistachios, watch scarlet cloud light wane across hill-huge sugarloaf domes eight hundred feet below me. Their sandstone hunks and hills and pinnacles are so sensually rounded as to make wind seem a voluptuary. Yet I'm grateful that the hot August wind of this afternoon has lulled to a breeze. And aside from the inevitable Southwestern gnats, no insects.

"Who needs pictographs?" I think, perhaps as a hedge against disappointment. "Summer evening, this canyon—they alone would be worth it." In case the rock art isn't? I grow dimly aware of an incongruity. On the doorsill of the twenty-first century, and a U.S. population poised for reveling in cyberspace, here I sit taking prehistoric relics for granted. By now, awake to that fact, sunset long gone, I find I'm sitting with a half moon in my lap.

ⓢ

Exhilarated by the good light of morning, I head down-trail into the canyon knowing memory hasn't deceived me: my passion for southeastern Utah is keen as ever. Knowing, too, that the rimrock trail I'm descending leads eventually to *big* pictographs, not mere doll-size, canyon-wall daubs. Along the so-called Great Gallery some virtually tower, I'm told: high as eight feet tall.

Fascinated by ancient things, I know those pictographs certainly qualify; they date back to somewhere between 500 B.C. and 500 A.D. True, that thousand-year "margin" of error seems enormous, but because radiocarbon dating won't work on rock art, a lot of it can't be dated at all. Even splitting the difference between the earliest and latest dates tells me I'm homing in on painted creatures whose lives began two thousand years ago!

Considering wind, weather, and bipeds, what's "surreal" is their survival. Painted in hardly more than colored mud patted or spattered onto bare rock, they owe their long lives to the arid Southwestern climate. And to the overhang of some cliff. And, equally vital, to human respect.

At the ruckus my boots make, yet another dust-colored whiptail scoots into its ankle-high bower of rabbit brush. Since both plant and lizard are ancient life-forms, if sheer antiquity triggers my affection, I should love them, too, shouldn't I? Fact is, I do. Whiptails have been for years my old reliables, my desert trail companions. "How ya doin'?" I say to this one. "Eating plenty of gnats for me? Attaboy. Keep up the good work."

Dipping into canyons you become a time diver who swims the geological past. If you begin under Utah's August-blue sky, you also dip into heat, the more the deeper, and perhaps descend further into the interrogative mood: "Are two quarts of water enough?"

For a mere seven miles they should be. I plan to check out the rock art then return, no dawdling. But even at 7:45 A.M. salty droplets keep smudging my sunglasses. My hatband rides on a film of sweat. My blue chambray shirt is soggy at the armpits, and under my light daypack its cotton is sopping.

"What if I get there and find those pictographs half-canceled by the chicken-scratching of vandals? Or greatly overrated? Or both?" Despite the hype by its devotees, very little rock art I've seen is "art." A lot of it is "Kilroy was here" stuff—at least to my eye. Plus, a shamefully large portion has indeed been vandal-struck.

"So," my quizzical side asks, "why bother?"

Maybe I just like the deep time of deserts. Back home in Boulder I drive past shopping complexes that seemingly weren't there a week ago. I pass suburbs that haven't yet lived long enough for a house cat to have died within them. But Southwestern canyons, especially those ungrazed by cattle, remain as they have been for thousands of years. Hallowed, almost, by time's weather? For me, yes. The high walls of this one with its sun-drenched sheernesses, its cougar-hued strata, and with its higher strata of fox-brown sandstone, and higher yet its glossy "varnish" of manganese oxide made indigo blue by the reflecting sky—all evoke the word "cathedral." Derisive skepticism even lets it stay there a full half-moment. Impressive, this canyon. Also hotter than hell.

🜚

The High Gallery would have been easy to miss. Not only are its pictographs, oh, maybe sixteen feet above the foot of their jagged eastward escarpment; they're in full shade—which is welcome—and take some squinting to make out. "Like clothespins!" I think.

Prosaic but true. The main figure, especially, which seems barely a yard long. His knobby head and round shoulders, the slim and armless torso of his red silhouette (if it is a he) are just like an old-fashioned, round clothespin. Except for *much* shorter legs, if that's what they are, and for the very unwooden way each painted shape seems to flow or hover: a whole array of such figures whose tapered silhouettes broaden toward the shoulders, like souls of red smoke, some twenty-seven or so.

But it's hard to say how many. Even the best preserved are a faded cranberry, while the faintest . . . well, they may not quite *be* there. Could be mere weather streaks. Nonetheless, a good two dozen— of what? Some sort of deities? Earth spirits? Sky spirits? Why so many, and why here? Because this place had been in some respect sacred? Nobody knows. All the same, it is. I know that much, or know it till my skeptical side asks why. And asks again, "Sacred? What's that supposed to mean?"

Out of squawbush to my left a dove flies up, making a whispering, half-whistling sound as it climbs.

From three dinky pools of rank water rises the mingled smell of black leaves and wet sand. By midsummer a few random pools are what's left of the stream. Which, when in spate, had wrapped great swatches of flotsam around cottonwood trunks near the streambed, grasses and twigs and dead branches half-woven together like the beginning of basketry. Over plump cobbles thirty feet away shuffles a badger looking stodgy and comic, paying me no mind whatever.

Those who painted such enigmatic figures saw the very things I'm seeing this minute. They relished this shade, breathed this morning air. Heard the stream speak in tongues when it flowed. Whoever painted them climbed down, hands reddened by hematite ground fine and mixed to a paste. He stood here looking up to appraise his work. As I'm doing now at stone wall become interface. Fellow earth. Across two thousand years that divide and unite us.

ᔥ

The Alcove, so called, is a typical cavelike niche at the foot of the canyon's west side. It yields surprise and dismay: lots more pictographs—cruder, mostly, yet easier to study by being shoulder high on their now fully sunlit wall—and greatly varied in design. But lightly marred, scratched over, alas, by among others, "Wick Read / 1928."

What brainless vanity! Even if he's still alive, and even if I owned a gun and could find him, I guess he'd be too old to deface. Have he and his ilk also slashed at the pictographs I most want to see?

That thought nudges my worry gland. I descend from the Alcove to continue down-canyon, weaving among hundreds of cottonwood and willow wands slender as arrows feathered with leaves—as if shot into the streambed's moist sand. Though in a scrub oak grove east of my route several mule deer browse on Indian rice grass, Easterners must otherwise puzzle: "What would possess Indians to live in a canyon?" Yet it's obvious that's where the water was, and is, when there is any. And shade. Up above you have a high, dry, mainly treeless plateau, compared to the oasis down here.

Fond of the passionate red put forth by claret-cup cactus, I bend low to examine one with blooms fully opened, anthers all pollen-flecked and expectant. It sums up the desert. Cacti may open their chests to show, like the heart of their mystery, a stunning red blossom, but every such disclosure is terribly well defended.

Always, Southwestern desert gives you little enough of one thing, more than enough of another. Mere pinches of soil, barren seven-league stretches of hardpan. Few and far between the cool shadows, sun everywhere blazing off blond or honey-colored walls and the waxy leaves of sparse cottonwoods. If those prehistoric peoples here before us looked squarely at this desert world and each other, yet loved them as this light so mercilessly shows things to be, they—by doing so—must've lived on the far side of some threshold we've long since crossed and forgotten.

Passing the clumped, sulphur-yellow abundance of chest-high rabbit brush in full bloom, I toss my head straight back for the few final droplets of one canteen—and get noon sun square in the eyes. Apart from the occasional box elder or cottonwood, shade during the next many hours will be scarce.

⑤

Arrival at the Great Gallery takes a while, even after I reach it. Its long smooth wall of spectral images, some pale as death, some intense as freshly dried blood, are unmistakable. Disappointing? Impressive? Actually, neither—at first, anyhow. Just very strange, and surprisingly *there*. But are they worth it? Worth the sweat and the miles? Beneath a cottonwood's merciful shade I flop down to study them, see what I think. Before I'm quite settled, though, I think, "Worth it? What a question!"

Either for painting or for viewing, no site could have been better. Not only does it afford a fifty-meter span of cliff wall, but much of the rock surface looks unusually smooth. At the base of that span, the stone has fractured so as to leave a fairly level terrace or pediment. That makes it easy to stroll the entire figural array close-up. First, though, I want the overall view. While some figures are small as a hand, most are unusually tall, and simple as a mummy's silhouette. Their lack of head-detail creates an ominous effect, except that some have been painted with eyes, which in a corpse seems especially weird. So maybe that's who they are, the venerable dead, open-eyed and wrapped for travel, legs bound together, arms tightly bound at their sides. But as if standing upright.

Floating might be a better term. Their earthen-red presences seem to levitate somewhere between the cliff surface and within its depths, making stone transparent. Several "mummies"—for that's indeed what they seem—show "internal" colors of mysterious design: faint green, white, pallid blue.

Even by sun dazzle they loom, specters that hover and say . . . something. Something otherworldly. Are they our oldest fears, archaic terrors alive in us still, panic-deep but made tolerable by projection as spirits? With the advantage of at least being placable by rite or sacrifice? So I guess but don't know. The experts call shapes like these "anthromorphs," but as to who left them here, specialists can only surmise and infer. They tell us that the painters lived before the Anasazi, thus were hunter-gatherers, ones called the "Barrier Canyon" people. So we know little more than these phantoms staring out from lost times choose to reveal.

ॺ

A lone hiker in just such canyons for many a year, I've been struck by the fact that solely as geological deposits the canyon escarpments seem awesome enough. Our geological sense, however, is barely two centuries old, whereas our primitive senses are ancient as blood coursing out of the mammalian past all the way here from the reptilian. Even in my eyes, erosional fractures and hulks often appear to be "other": now some sort of giant, now an ogre. Once seen like that, reason doesn't quite dispel them—not entirely. Though reason forces those grotesquely animate features back to being just stone, an afterimage of the creature that seemed to glower or forebode dimly persists. Naturally the mind smiles at its own childish apprehensions. Then smiles again, more humbly, realizing how much more natural fear is than reason. The aspect of mind called "blood" is a thousand ten thousand times older.

Well, if one's "enlightened" psyche can still feel naked sandstone coming somewhat alive, how much more intensely, irresistibly pre-historic minds must've felt the same. In drawing our present line between living things and those we think of as not having life, we humans were fearfully slow. To do it took millennia beyond know-ing, and I've a hunch we haven't drawn it right even yet.

Along the sandier, more open reaches, shadows of sagebrush and shadscale bushes begin to lengthen. Dimples in trodden sand take on an indigo tint. Up out of sight and out of hearing along the rim, piñon jays will soon chatter and gather like static, scolding rivals away from favorite boughs. I hadn't supposed I'd stay much more than half an hour, and here I've spent the whole afternoon, fasci-nated. And spent all but a last one or two medium gulps in my sec-ond canteen.

Meanwhile, a hitherto dismissive opinion of rock art as "art" has softened. The more I look, the more my curiosity tinges with re-spect. If we judge "art" by its emotional power, these eerie creatures have plenty of that. A power I for once don't care to analyze, only receive. Sometimes, instead of my gazing at them, they turn the ta-bles on me: I'm the one looked at. So steadily, so ominously, they partly translate me to whatever, whoever they are. As if I'd been summoned.

Had I come across them in Greece or Italy I'd say they stood waiting for Charon, the ferryman of the dead. But no, they've al-ready crossed the river Styx. They stand waiting for me to come, cross over to them. So after years of intending to look upon these very forms, my arrival becomes a vague departure. Toward a sodal-ity of red shadows. How the last, long breath of an entire people might appear in dream.

Exactly that. Momentarily, they're in the same dream I am, imag-ining myself already in theirs. Here in remote desert that most city dwellers would scorn as "the middle of nowhere," a stone panel re-veals to me some forty ghosts who summarize all of us, the living and the dead, past and to come. Earlier I had thought, "red smoke."

This setting makes that phrase terribly apt. Straight up, straight up above the Barrier Canyon people, therefore above us, too, impends one massively brute and beautiful crush, stratum stacked atop stratum. A highest ledge jutting out exactly above "the people" is battleship thick. When it falls, as it must. . . .

Hunks and overhangs aren't "the truth," exactly. Stone tons are just facts. Truth can only be human. When set off by pathos as painted by our cousins, the Barrier Canyon ones, however, those stone facts become—if not "the truth"—implacably true. But the painters of such grave, rouge-tinted figures couldn't have had any glimmer of that, could they? Couldn't have known the score in *that* manner? Mere primitives?

In any case, I'm one of their number. Sharing an August sun they too had to tighten their eyes against, when its glare picked out every dint or bit of nubble on this tawny smoothness of wall. So for as long as Indian eyes and eyes like mine have been coming here, the sky has been both Utah-blue and dark as a rock's insides, has been sunfire and daylight petrified.

Certainly these forms prove museums woefully artificial. If you detached even the tallest, most ornate of them to be tastefully floated two inches off some gallery wall—well, no amount of subdued Hopi flute music would allow them to be seen as themselves: archaic, profound, apparitional.

Here, only here, in their natal canyon can they be what they are: far taller than I am, but given the cliff's towering verticality, they're thin, minuscule, powerless. Yet as profound, too, as all the daybreaks and moonrises, all the summer rains and winter snows they've been presiding over for two thousand years. Because isn't that what they've been doing down through those lonely centuries: being true to themselves? And true to us.

I'm not alone in feeling so.

Taking up a steno pad that the National Park Service has placed on site, I leaf through penciled reactions, pages of them, set down by others who've experienced this pictographic display. Many entries comment on the canyon's beauty. Others angrily denounce vandals of rock art. Many praise the Park Service for helping keep that to a minimum. "Worth the trip from Rochester to see this panel," says one. Others have come from as far as Australia, not to mention Canton, Ohio, and Berne, Switzerland, and Belgium, Japan, South Africa. From all over.

Most entries dated "July" mention heat. In a child's block printing, Marie Talkington of Spokane says, "Had a great hike, spotted 4 deer, 10 lizards, o snakes. The hottest day of my life. Very pretty, lots of bees and bugs, but nice for taking pitchers. I would grade it way cool."

Another kid, a week later, grumps dissent: "We are from Brooklyn and all seven of us are sitting here in the heat and I am ten years and I am very very very hot. My mom told us to go here and I am dying here my mom forced me and I wish I had ice cream and I wish I had a very cold water and I wish I was at Brooklyn."

For some the hike was strenuous, for others a cakewalk. One entry gripes there aren't enough trail cairns, which the following entry pooh-poohs: "You couldn't miss the turns unless you had your eyes closed." Baron and Crista from Klamath Falls, Oregon, advise against making things easy: "Keep the road unimproved, keep limiting the access, otherwise it'll be another Mesa Verde."

The thirst motif recurs when a kid signing just "Nicholas" speaks his need by drawing a man and a woman, each holding *large* bottles marked WATER, but adds, "I like this place a lot." Then in a P.S., "The mule deer try to hide, but I can see them."

Other signees use few words. "Wonder full" and "Unbelievably amazing and beautiful!" and "So spiritual!" and "A religious experience" and "No words, just wonder." That word "spiritual" strikes a note sounded more often than any other, as when Susan Ward of Walnut Creek, Connecticut, says, "Moving ghosts gave off a scary, unknowing feeling. What does this really mean?" Clint Nathrop of

Idalia, Illinois, echoes that: "This spot leaves me with a feeling of mystical awe! What a privilege!"

These reactions occur to Liz Sammartino of Canton, Ohio, who begins similarly by rising tiptoe: "Amazing! To have lived at this time, the enjoyment and the freedom they must have had," she goes on; then redeems sentimentality with "and I'm sure much sorrow." Yes, surely much of that. Especially in desert, hunter-gatherers live and die by a single season of rain, not to mention sickness, reptiles, vermin, broken bones, hostile raids.

Yet no amount of reverence can replace the fluid that Utah's radiance sweats out of us. "Good to be here," says an unsigned entry, "but I wish I was back at the truck for a beer." Left with only a swallow or so of water for my hike out, I'd rather not think about beer. As his early-morning sign-in on July 20, however, a ranger had written: "Today's going to be another roaster," making thirsty thoughts hard to avoid. Next day must've been torrid also, because on July 21 Heidi from Wiesbaden, Germany, had made her entry a penciled sigh: "Water would be nice."

Nothing plaintive, though, about the surprise announcement by Jill Klexner and her new spouse: "Today is day 3 of our married life. Honeymoon in Horseshoe Canyon." Its spell has evidently acted on others similarly, as attested by P. Wilson and Frank Cooley, who wrote: "We met here 3 years ago and were married a year later. Someone 10,000 years back decided we needed a special place to start. We'll return."

"Return?" Pondering that, I find myself nodding, "Me, too."

"But you've been here, done this," says my logical side. "You've just spent *hours* gazing. Why come again?"

"Oh, I gazed all right," comes my answer. "And in a way almost spoke with them, too. Or at least listened."

Spoke with them or with something. With the spirit of place, possibly. Meaning their spirits? The Barrier Canyon people? Meaning my spirit in theirs? As usual, I don't really know. Oh, I *know*. The dead have only the voices we lend them. Nor could pictographs, however ancient, have put me in touch with dwellers of a canyon called "the other world." I know—or think I do—that such a world is reachable only in this one. Terrain of the real surreal: where something not a "thing" nor even myself seems part of the talking.

Early as next summer, perhaps, or surely the one after, my inner critic may agree that's reason enough to come back: for the conversation.

ᔕ

Having taken longer than planned, I've a thirsty trail ahead of me, up to the rim, but enjoy the sun's longer shadows. And violet-green swallows beginning their daredevil evening feed. I become half-entranced watching my boot toes scatter sand, each stride kicking ahead a delicate, parabolic spray. Sand not yet stone, though it has been and will be again.

At a blossoming stalk I'm delayed a longish while by wondering what it is. Nothing I've seen, not even in field guides. The whole plant is encrusted coral-thick with blossoms small as a shirt-button. It stands slightly above knee-high, with a treelike structure, but instead of green stalk, each thin branch is prodigiously bloom-clustered in florets like micro-hollyhocks or tiny roses of Sharon. From each minute petal's outer tissue, eggshell white, lines finer than eyelash lead down into a calyx of rose-hip red. Every stalk is a-burst with enthusiasm bespeaking Nature's careful and lavish sides at once. Never have I seen anything either more beautiful or astonishing, because *where* it flowers is part of what it is. Yet in all that extravagant expense of petals on a single plant, nothing Nature spends is spent.

Continuing up trail I'm bemused. Why should a single blossoming plant simply ravish me? I mean, why, beyond its obvious beauty, should I continue being haunted by it? The exuberance of its blooms? Their profusion? My knowing nothing about it, thus ignorance made mystery? Those were factors, but hardly explained the depth of my reaction. Surely I had sensed that the plant's beauty and exuberance were more than just related to place *where*. As if those profuse florets and the canyon were somehow part of each other.

With that awareness came a hint as to why I'd long wanted to visit those pictographs—a hint that my distrust of sentimentality hadn't admitted. The appeal of the Barrier Canyon rock art surely had had *some*thing to do with oneness, the oneness of an ancient people and place. I had wanted to touch that wholeness, that integrity, of a people whose fates had given them a harsh, arid, merciless land to make do with, and who had found it beautiful, and who, whatever their shortcomings, had loved it with all their hearts.

Citizen of a nation where, for all too many of us, no lake, plain, plateau, river, or forest is more precious than what can be done to them or made out of them; born into a culture where all too often the only sacrament is money, I had come to this canyon—in part, anyhow—to visit a people among whom the earth was never for sale. A sort of kinship? To go that far . . . well, "sentimental" would be the kindest thing you could say.

Nonetheless, and perhaps naturally, I'm by now seeing late afternoon in the canyon as they, "the people," would have seen it. Trying to. On whimsical impulse I begin "recognizing" this or that lizard along the trail as one of the Barrier Canyon people in cunning disguise. I try catching a whiptail, knowing I can't. It's just that I'm amused by how quickly they dart and scoot, and how tantalizingly close they allow my hand to come. Then gone, skedaddled! Even the youngest—barely three inches, tail and all, thus presumably less wily than their elders—easily elude me. With a sudden flick, each leaves my fingers snatching at tawny dust exactly matching their skin.

As the trail rises, switchback on switchback, the canyon floor recedes further into blue shadow. Much of its way now ascends over bare stone littered with shale of a coffee-bean brown, bits of which make grinding crunches under boot soles.

In mountains, eight hundred feet of ascent isn't worth talking about, and I'm used to mountains; perhaps it's thirst slowing my stride to a daydreamy trudge. Entries from that steno pad keep coming to mind, almost as voices. For frankness, of course, my favorite had to be the Brooklyn kid, just as for hardihood I must admire any girl who finds the hottest day of her life "nice for taking pitchers." For humane insight, though, I savor Liz Sammartino's phrase, "and I'm sure much sorrow," which recalls the apprehensive note of her closing words: "I hope people remember this is spiritual ground and not to ruin it."

Though wishfulness isn't my style, on reading her hope half like a prayer, I had felt something in me say, "Amen," as I do now, remembering. Even my rationalist side sees the logic: If you believe there's such a thing as desecration, you believe in the sacred.

A Twist of Rope at Yellow Jacket

Time has taken many shapes at our hands, with some of the oldest, most humble remaining very much our contemporaries. Pot. Sandal. Knife. Twine. Such everyday yet unchanging faces of human invention have always fascinated me. Their shapes proved from the first so naturally apt as to hardly have altered over who knows how many migrations Paleolithic, and now ours, and still we can't do without them. The basket, for example. Or the coat, which may well have begun as a robe also a blanket. And rope: plain, everyday, age-old, indispensable rope.

Last evening, in poor light, I leaned toward a bit of rope uncovered by Dr. Joe Ben Wheat, an archaeologist who for several decades supervised excavations of the large Anasazi village at Yellow Jacket in southwestern Colorado. Buried years had darkened its fibers to umber but hadn't impaired their familiar twist. Sun-tanned and shirtless, young archaeology students went past me loading trays of cataloged relics into a van, but I got one student to hold on a moment while I took a quick look.

Even in the fast-waning glimmers of summer twilight I saw enough to wonder at. Woven around A.D. 1100, its strands—except for their darkened color and some crumpling—seemed identical to store-bought rope I'd used that very morning when cinching an ice chest tighter to the bed of my pickup. Dusk thickened even as I bent forward, so whether the Anasazi specimen had been woven of yucca fibers or juniper bast, I couldn't be sure, but no matter. Nor did it matter that my own rope had been hemp, not yucca. It and the Anasazi rope of nine centuries ago were all but twins.

Why should I be flabbergasted that at Mesa Verde a large hank of yucca cord found "admirably well-preserved and extremely strong" measures more than 1,300 feet? Why, in the museum there, when I first stood before a display featuring similar cord, did I find myself leaning forward, incredulous? The tightness and fineness that somebody's gone hands had imparted to mere yucca fibers hadn't seemed possible. Yet there it was, right under my nose. Its excellence demanded that I upgrade my sense of the prehistoric mind. But I'm not alone in finding that change hard to make, as if some hidden resistance inside the adjective "prehistoric" were a drag on so doing. "That long ago," I kept thinking, "and yet so tight, so right. With such *quality!*"

I know. That doesn't add up, isn't logical. Regarding cordage skills alone it isn't, much less on weaving, pottery, agriculture. My brain admits it. The brain remembers, too, that an excavation at White Dog Cave brought back into Arizona sunlight a game-entangling net of twine whose meshwork measures 237 feet long by a yard wide. Which doesn't stop my cognitive organ from feeling that "prehistoric" connotes, however subtly, "inferior."

My hands know better. Know that if their lives depended on working cord half so fine into a net anything like that "prehistoric" one, I'd be in for a desperate apprenticeship. In even a best-case scenario my hands foresee ten very bony fingers by the end.

Back in Boulder, where I bought the rope in my truck, there's an atomic clock whose hyperaccurate atom of cesium gives off or absorbs a photon at intervals so periodically precise we gasp. On the other hand, rope humbles our technological pride a notch by reminding us that despite our making a clock out of atomic changes in matter, there may have been little change in what really matters. The very lab housing that clock uses miles of rope in lashing equipment onto trucks and in roping off grounds under construction.

Through a simple twist given coarse fibers, our world is still tied to that of the Anasazi, and to worlds long before theirs. Among time's everyday shapes, rope is merely an instance. Pot. Sandal. Knife. Beads. Walking stick. No end to our beginnings.

The Tree beyond Imagining

Seeing is not believing. Any tree "acting out" in such hog-wild and crazy ways—or so I used to feel—can't be truly arboreal. This one thinks it's a mad dog. Here's another trying to prove chaos might be a conifer. Yet another so cleft and warped it looks like self-knowledge. Or is it just pretending to summarize World History?

Botanically speaking, of course, a juniper can't be perverse. As a dirt-common member of the cypress family it can at worst be only an oddball conifer. Other arboreal species may echo states we recognize in ourselves, but none I've run across seems so moody and emotional. Lifelong, we humans conceal our intimate histories, even while a version of them gets slowly written into our faces. This tree's neurotic past, however, appears at a glance, visible through no matter how many feigned identities. Admittedly, cone-bearing trees in general may be tricky to tell apart, one from another, not to mention the taxonomic hair-splitting you'd need for identifying some *sixty* species of juniper, but recognizing the desperate types I have in mind is easy.

First you see billowing curds and clouds of green needles on twigs wispy as string and nearly as limp. Those "needles," however, have evolved to minuscule scales, glossy green and trimly overlapping. Evolution has also downsized the juniper's cones to virtual berries. Yet each berrylike cone retains tiny nibs, corners almost, as if hinting their spheres remember once being otherwise. Beneath erstwhile needles now smoother than snakeskin, and under cones shrunk to beads, a grayish-brown welter of wood appears. If it looks like tensed muscle and sinew, that illusion and the preceding traits do add up to generic juniper. But if the bark is shaggy as hanks of unbraided sisal, if the absolutely motionless trunk seems to be groveling or smoke, and if in even the best-behaved specimen you see branches that mime Devastation having a temper tantrum, you know you're not only dealing with *Juniperus osteosperma,* Utah juniper—you know the example before your eyes is a special case: a high-desert strain of that species, one growing where it ought not to try.

If animal, such trees would be camels, and almost are. But what camel drinks sand? Hence the near incredulity. On a sun-spattered, all-but-windless morning in Utah, for example, you stand smack in front of one, gasping at its self-tormented trunk fed by red sand or far less: a crevice in rock once sand. Yet on naked stone those knotted roots have knuckled down to sipping a trunk and limbs into life. From a low branch you might strip off a fibrous dangle of bark the creature seems clad in, all threads and shreds and tatters, like a beggar's rags. Obviously the bark's stringy hairs are real. Just as clearly, its tree *as tree* lacks full credibility. The riven trunk, the gesturing limbs in every style of passion, cannot be anything Nature approves, much less intended.

That's why, in your earliest encounters with Utah juniper—and especially if you've seen how Tuscan farmers cleave and otherwise torture olive trunks into yielding larger crops along their terraced groves—you're bound to wonder about botanical vandalism. Novicelike, you stand there in southeastern Utah just staring and shaking your head: "Surely someone has *done* this?"

Surely yes. Such a juniper-storm of contortion must have been *caused.*

When it was only a seedling, had an off-road vehicle run it over? Had it been trompled by a grazing steer? On his "timber-splitter" of a cowhorse had some nineteenth-century ranch hand ridden it down? Or, because junipers can easily be many hundred years old, had some Spanish explorer whacked away with his axe? Plain as sunlight, the tree half standing, half disheveling before you cannot in the course of nature have become what it is.

But trying to make that view fit entire swaths of them is so ridiculous you're forced to discard your vandalism theory almost before it forms. Nonetheless, a lingering suspicion may recur, insisting that no tree unmolested would grow as this one before you has. The postures vary too greatly for wind to explain them. Wind produces a leaning *away* from, as with Monterey cypress along the California shore, or timberline trees in Rocky Mountain high country. Where prevailing currents distort trees, you see unanimity. They all know in their bones which way the wind blows, so on that they agree without dissent. Besides, what wind could pretzel a trunk?

In the earliest phase of my fascination, however, conjectures of human abuse often wrestled a moment with something a lot older than botany. Even now, my absent-minded look at one or another extravagant specimen can revive animism without half trying. Animism's primitive belief that each thing—cloud, pebble, cave, or lake—is enspirited might as well have sprung from the same seed as Utah juniper.

More than once, in me anyhow, it has given that archaic belief a new twist. Especially at dusk, moving through a forest of high-desert juniper while forgetting our century (and myself as a child of its science), I've often, for six or eight milliseconds, gone backward in time. Have turned primitive enough for a juniper's spirit to take over mine. Then, with a smile (or blush) of self-exorcism, my awareness would shake off that twilight tree-soul.

Not with a shudder. I've always liked the idea of being a tree, though without bothering much about what kind. Modesty prevents even thinking "sequoia," of course. Aspens are lovely yet giddy, their leaves having such a short attention span. Lodgepole pine? No, too thicksown amid themselves ever to let understory bushes grow at their feet. "All of us," they seem to say, "and none of you." Douglas fir are less clannish but seem honor-bound forever to stand at attention, whereas blue spruce prefer to be comfortable. My respect for stamina, as in hackberry and Gambel oak, doesn't mean I'd go to extremes by becoming one of Utah's more cantankerous junipers. They've enough hardihood to make me half worship them, true; but just looking at one feels like work. A single day of *being* such a Gordian gnarl would exhaust me. That's why, whenever a juniper's soul tries getting possession of mine, I'm never so flattered as to abandon the actual. We survive by knowing our limits.

§

Fact is, for Utah juniper of the high desert, flabbergasting abnormality is the norm only among individual trees defying limitation. Lots of rock, lots of sand, lots of wind, and very little rain can make juniper stands growing there, at the far end of possibility, an outpost of marginalized eccentrics. Not the whole species. No, the stressed-out examples I'm talking about, the trees you can see without quite believing, grow where they almost can't—at their ecological edge. We think timberline a question of mountain altitudes beyond which no conifer can rise. For desert junipers timberline may be a threshold drawn in the sand, not by rarefied air but by rain—lower than which there is none, or as good as. Which makes this plant standoffish, like desert flora generally. The more arid the clime, the more space between survivors.

"Between competitors" puts that same desert fact differently. Botanists speak of this juniper as "intolerant" of shade, but that apparent disadvantage may be a strength. It keeps offspring from growing up at home, lest their roots rival the parent tree in its questing for moisture. Viable cones that want to become trees, therefore, need to hope a bird or coyote will deign to swallow them. Animals can't digest the cone's seeds, only excrete them, probably far from the parent tree where they have almost no chance anyhow. So the boughs of Utah junipers often seem simply drenched with berrylike cones, each holding three seeds.

But that's nature—always spending far too much, so as to spend enough. It's also desert life, which judging from innumerable juniper cadavers strewn over the desert floor, quite a few die trying to live. Yet I'll not describe their mummified trunks in any detail; not how the exposed, bark-lorn grain bleaches gray, then blackens; nor describe how, after long, sun-riddled exposure, that grain delaminates and splays open; nor emphasize the crackle and pop of shattered twigs, eerie as brittle bones, stepped on, when you walk round such a trunk to inspect it. Saying that those defunct junipers remind me of war casualties would seem exaggeration enough; actually, though, they always remind me of atrocities: of passionate creatures made to die by inches, and in pain unspeakable. I have felt that for years, with no thought of writing about it, nor have those years changed my reaction. It's as unbidden as it is invariable. I cannot *not* feel for them. Sadly, I look down at their death throes and shake my head, as if at inflictions so cruel the torturers *had* to be human.

One most notable aspect, however, I must dwell on: how the fallen trunks lie, twisted as they grew, like a washcloth wrung dry. I've found those with torsos turned a full 360 degrees in less than seven inches of length! When I photograph examples, it's not because I suppose nobody will believe me; a month later, I may not believe myself.

If not so common, any stress-ridden Utah juniper would be a museum piece. Actually, I've never visited a collection of rarities offering anything that astonishing, yet so common that it covers vast stretches of Arizona, Nevada, Utah, and into western Colorado. Despite those millions of junipered acres, though, even if you could somehow uproot one, loosening its rockbound grip on desert life, then put it in a museum . . . the credibility gap would widen to a chasm. Few people unfamiliar with Southwestern flora would believe *that* example untampered with. Like you, they'd murmur to themselves, "This isn't nature's work. It must be some kind of hoax." At the very least, they'd think it a mutant so atypical of its species as to have been displayed solely for its shock value.

ெ

Thus, it's by taking root at the threshold of impossibility that this most irrational tree grows against all reason, to fit any shape of amazement. Compulsively so. By contrast, the lumber industry would welcome a wholly reasonable tree: *Arbor sapiens,* maybe, or *Arbor cogitans.* It would grow erect, straight-grained, knot-free; but if gene-splicing scientists ever set out to contrive it, they couldn't do better than to plunk themselves down in front of the oldest, most outlandish Utah juniper discoverable—so as to engender its opposite. Meanwhile, my favorites are those barely good for even themselves, much less for wood products, unless bent toothpicks and shaggy matches should come into fashion. As one forestry expert puts it, such a tree is "unmerchantable." Sawmills wouldn't know where to begin. Or why.

Repeatedly I have stood before a Utah juniper and felt unable to make sense of it, literally couldn't tell if I were looking at one tree or two or several. Couldn't see where its, or their, main limbs either began or ended. I have climbed into them, the better to discern exactly that little. No wonder. At the edge of its range, it is either so distraught or far gone in perplexity it can't make sense of itself. "Do you suppose I'd have grown this way," it seems to snort, "if I'd had any idea what I was getting into?" Its confusion is echoed by botanists, who categorize the species as "a shrub or small tree." But which? As a rule of thumb, trees are plants you can walk under. To do that with most examples of *Juniperus osteosperma,* you'd have to duck for part of the way and tunnel the rest. There are plenty of indisputable trees—blue spruce, to name one—offering similar obstruction. Then, too, on seeing a plant tall as any giraffe, and with trunks a foot or two thick, we're disinclined to say "shrub."

On second thought, although the specimens I admire would indeed make more interesting museum pieces than many a prize now under glass, I realize that bringing just the tree inside wouldn't do. You'd need to bring along with it the thin air of its Southwestern plateau. You'd need, too, that powdery fine sand red as rust, rippled dunes sparsely tufted with greasewood or Indian rice grass. And skies blue as chicory petals. Floating puffs of cumulus, too, their slow undersides tinted by the red miles beneath them. Birdsong as well: rock wrens, horned larks, mockingbirds, vireos, piñon jays. And scrub jays, cowbirds, towhees. And vultures. Above all, you'd need desert sun with its glare, its incomparable clarities, deep shadows. Its refusal to lie.

§

Such a maverick plant looks unlikely for any useful purpose, but on the often rock-naked hardpan of Arizona, for example, where we might say "nothing here" or "pure desolation," Indians saw in junipers food, firewood, weaving material, building supplies, and even medicine. Millennia of desert necessity taught Indians, present-day and prehistoric, to explore every last one of the juniper's possibilities.

Mere minutes of hands-on experience can suggest at least a couple. Take the tree's inner bark. You've but to work it a moment to see how easily it goes all to pieces, making it a natural tinder. For Indians, of course, that's some of what it was: fire-starter, a wad of which would be carried in the same buckskin pouch with flints, or kept with the firebow and drill. But the inner bark was good for more than tinder. When rubbed to a fine frazzle, it became diapers for infants, bedding for cradle boards, bedding for invalids, menstrual cloths, dressing for wounds. Braided, its fibers turned to rope. Though the Anasazi usually wove their sandals of yucca leaves, I've come upon bits and pieces of juniper-bark sandal left by them. Unwoven and sparingly mixed with clay, the same bark helped adobe bind to willow-wand partitions and freestone interiors. Moreover, though Anasazi pottery used clay tempered with crushed stone or sherds, juniper fibers seem to have been occasionally used instead.

Examples of bark-laced adobe occur in many Utah canyons and across the Southwest. Over those clay-plastered walls I've seen hundreds of juniper roof-traves. In sandstone caves I've come to expect, along with the usual potsherds and corn cobs, flecks of charcoal left many centuries ago by the Anasazi, who burnt juniper for cooking and warmth. Not knowing what the world's most fragrant firewood may be, I do know that at campsites throughout Utah, New Mexico, and Arizona my nostrils have inhaled juniper smoke like incense. Navajos still use it for hogans, firewood, corrals, cradle boards. Hopis rely on it, too, as do Pueblos generally, both for daily living and their year-cycle of ceremonies. To this hour, nobody travels the Four Corners area without seeing juniper palings, fenceposts, and stock pens wherever people are or have been, because it's a wood too stubborn not to take its time about rotting.

Then there's juniper-as-sustenance. Its so-called berries have long been eaten by humans and animals . . . and, every season, one or two are eaten by me. Edibility varies depending on species and on whom you talk to. One modern authority says "not actually inedible." Hardly an endorsement. In my view, "edibility" depends on your being ten days into starvation. An old proverb says hunger's the best sauce. Add the berries' eye appeal, often considerable, and your hand would reach out to them, their blue haze smudging from under the thumb like the breath of yeast on a grape, a blue lovely and thin as air on a planet.

So much for looks. Analysis of Rocky Mountain juniper, *Sabina scopulorum,* reveals "a high percentage of sugar," but if it's there, it's hiding from me. Crush a berry off either that species or a Utah juniper and your thumb and forefinger will smell vaguely of gin. Sucking on the same berry's strongly resinous pulp, you taste broad hints of turpentine. Yet we know Indians ate juniper berries raw, boiled, and roasted. Taking dried berries from their winter stores, they sometimes ground them into a consistency mealy enough for a sort of juniper-berry gruel or for patting into cakes. Ash from burning the scale-like needles could flavor boiling water, which, strained of sediment, pepped up other foods.

Even then, Indian resourcefulness wasn't exhausted. The berries' waxy coating could be boiled off and skimmed for rubbing into leather, bowstrings, cordage, what have you. Roasted berries were ground between two stones for making a sort of Indian coffee. Apparently a medicinal, tea-like decoction was made from young shoots. Junipers also provided jewelry. Navajos still collect the pebble-hard seed within each berry for drilling then stringing with tiny glass beads of various colors.

༄

Within the so-called mystery of life the greater mystery is will. Why should life *will* to be, and with such perseverance? Why has life fought so intensely long and cleverly against taking "No!" for its answer? Where rock and sand and desert conditions seem to echo an indifferent cosmos, seem to virtually demand that one or another seedling give in to the forces *against* life, a juniper may buckle and distort like anguish itself but refuse to throw in the sponge—as if to say, "I wouldn't give them the satisfaction!"

Maybe that's why, roving the Grand Canyon's South Rim, I have spent hours of clear weather more intrigued by its pygmy forest of piñons and junipers than by the view. Yes, that canyon's an erosional wonder, but it's a triumph of gravity, of force pulling in the downward direction, whereas life strives upward. The opposite way.

There, happily stumbling over outcrops of chert and Kaibab limestone, well content at being scolded by piñon jays, I have come upon deep depression and recovery—both alive in the same tree. How had it grown so depressed? Through wrestling for its own affections? Or was it too much a shape-shifter ever to tire of dilemma? And how had recovery and relapse spread from the same trunk? Because its moods (like ours) don't believe in each other? There I found trees giving instructions in bravery. Found them more typical than not. To look at such lives and say "struggle" doesn't touch it.

During that same afternoon I came upon the very juniper who, once it discovered witchcraft, couldn't quit practicing; then found countless others its bad example converted. As if they had used forbidden spells to demand eternal life *and* youth, they seemed the picture of what happens when only the first half is granted, the picture of how losers look when they win.

There amid the deranged and violent I also discovered "good" trees battening on the same rimrock; witnessed all the living optimism, all the hurt joy that can scuffle upward out of such rock and suffer openly. In wresting a living from limestone's long famines of rain, they must sometimes have felt that enduring there was next to impossible, but endure they had.

We admire most, I suppose, those virtues our souls utterly lack, or need more of. Even after twenty years, therefore, I'm apt to be spellbound by the drama of a particular trunk and limbs. My feeling sympathy and awe before such pure indomitability costs nothing, I admit; yet I've often stood so, and often a longish while, unaware that I was. As if hoping a touch of juniper courage might agree to come with me.

Newspaper Rock and the Idiot Race

Utah, along Indian Creek. A large slab, darkened by desert varnish, swarms with petroglyphs in such variety it's called Newspaper Rock. Spirals, arrows, desert bighorn. Antlered shamans. Handprints. Stick-figure lizards. "Journey lines" tracing, it is thought, the ancient route taken by some clan. Six-toed footprints, quite a few. Horseback Indians with bow and arrow. All teem the slab's surface, dozens and dozens of them, pecked through the darkness of manganese oxide to reveal sandstone's light brown. Oldest among these images are ones estimated to have been left there fifteen centuries ago!—whereas those showing horses may be as recent as two hundred years. The effect, I must say, is a delight and a babble, like tongues of lost languages all speaking at once, tantalizing viewers with mysterious utterance right under their noses.

Among them are images not a bit puzzling, scars that pistol-packing vandals have added, ones their gunfire smacked into that sandstone panel. Before civilization by rednecks, its strange symbols had endured how many rains, blizzards, hailstorms?

Such brainless blazing away at petroglyphs, some estimated to have lasted longer than the Roman empire, evokes for me the very voice of an English historian I knew in my student years. He was such an incomparably nimble-witted and charming Brit that talk shows literally sent limousines for him. During one of our strolls together through a sculpture garden, he drew my attention to some vandalism there, then had belied his buoyantly energetic manner by remarking bitterly that our own historical time is "the era of the idiot race." He meant it etymologically: in ancient Greek, *idiotes* describes one who is private, apart. Thus an "idiot race" would consist of alienated people who see themselves as neither part of the past, nor of society as a whole, nor of any shared respect.

Back then, I had smiled with all the sagacity of my twenty-four years and told that distinguished Fellow of All Souls College, Oxford, his "Age of the Idiot" was mere cynicism. In turn he had wryly twitted me on my "very American optimism" and let it go at that.

Wherever the Anasazi past has been left unguarded, which is mostly, *idiotes* have dilapidated kivas, artifacts, petroglyphs, and even pictographs. A form of pollution, and of the pleasurable power felt in destroying—a very real pleasure indeed. Here in the West, for example, how many road signs out of ten lack bullet holes? We look to such highway signs for information, and get more than we want. Blunt as slugs, the riddled ones tell where we are, how far we still have to go. Do those gunfire "glyphs" dimpling Newspaper Rock offer the same? Are they too "the news"?

Now a generation older than when I strolled chattily alongside my historian elder, I hope I'm wise enough to change my mind, but on "the era of the idiot race" I haven't. True, our U.S. population has more than doubled since I was twenty-four, which means we've at least twice as many idiots, in the Greek sense, or—given the spread of alienation—many times twice as many. That's scary, but enough for a whole "era" of them? Admittedly, road signs and such are replaceable, whereas ancient images are not. Once destroyed, their prehistoric gestures won't reappear.

Nonetheless, the good news is this: all manner of decent people visit the Anasazi past, countless thousands every season, awestruck by paradox: relics of great age, yet so defenseless and fragile.

Trouble is, the reverence paid by no matter how many thousands remains utterly invisible. Then, devoid of respect or anything like it, along comes the comparatively rare bit of bad news. It comes on two legs: a pothunter or vandal *idiotes*. Of his kind it takes only one. One only. That's the sadness.

Sound of Nowhere

Mountains echo whatever you tell them, but desert space is always a listener, its only voice a quiet so unbroken it hushes *you,* thereby making you fit to enter in.

Often for long moments even your know-it-all, factual, busy-body self stops chattering. Without the slightest intention, you may find you've slowed your walk to a standstill, then stopped. You may find you've stood two, three minutes amid the quietudes of desert space. Not moving, just listening. But listening to what? To breeze through your wide-brimmed straw hat? To the stir of Mormon tea bushes, whose leaves are green stems? To the drift of small, puffy clouds overhead? To nothing?

To that, yes. Nothing at all. Yet something. More than a millennium and a half ago, amid the rocks and sands of Egypt, the Desert Fathers heard it, too. A refreshment. A silence that draws the soul.

Waking from that half-trancelike state, you know you've heard something that still can't be bottled, machined, plasticized, taped, drilled, stockpiled, freeze-dried, databased, downloaded, circulated, replayed, or otherwise "captured for loved ones." But if one iota of such thoughts could occur to you while hearing "nothing," you wouldn't be hearing it. You'd be that diminished thing: yourself. How delicious, instead, to listen and be no one at all. A "no one" brimful, an emptiness who has *become* what there is.

Even in desert space, however, such moments aren't anything

you can command, make happen. Within them, you recover how it feels to be completely alive without trying. Without thought, too, as we think of it, but far from mindless. Just here and nowhere. The center place.

The Pleasures of Ruin

He was a big fellow, 6'3" if an inch, and built like an NFL lineman, somewhat paunchy but with muscle beneath.

"Looking for Jailhouse?" I asked as he headed straight toward it and me.

"Yeah," he said, without much enthusiasm.

By late June in Utah's red-rock country, the mind never strays far from water and shade in heat making it hard to enjoy one without the other. Turkey vultures cruise the hot blue, usually gliding on energy the sun has supplied via convection. What clouds there are float on their backs, never their bellies, as if they love drifting face toward the sun while the rest of us sweat.

"You camped up the canyon?" I asked, assuming—since he carried only a light daypack—he'd come from just round the bend.

"Naw," he said. "Me and my wife's day-hiking. We're parked up to Sheik's Flat."

My eyes widened. He'd already scrambled five miles down pour-offs, around boulders big as small hills, up steep parts, then again down, joltingly, over boulder-choked "trail" like a dynamiter's idea of how to imitate chaos, past places where every so often you stand a quarter-minute, deciding, then proceed, a handhold and foothold at a time. Even if he went no farther than this site, he and his wife had all that to do again in reverse. Red-rock trekkers disagree which is easier, the getting down into, or the climbing back out. My legs generally find it's the one I'm not doing at the time.

"All the way here," I asked, "mainly for this one?"

"Oh, we looked at a ruin or two while we were at it," he said. "Shot some petroglyphs and stuff." The heavy telephoto zoom on his old-style Minolta implied interest in rock art. Then into view behind him came a woman, surely his wife, contouring along that same ledge. Lean and tall, with her dark ponytail hanging down over a T-shirt tucked into denim cut-offs, she too stepped with a methodical rhythm instilled by that trail and the hot sky's solar radiance. Eastward across the canyon, swifts hustled, plunged, and rolled away on air.

Joining us, she must have uttered more than "Hi." Now, though, four years after, I remember not a word. The hushabye singsong of gusty wind in those junipers said more than they. His manner wasn't so much unsociable as monosyllabic. To each other they spoke even less than to me. Clearly, however, legging it down here had been *his* idea.

Well, because it's my nature, because people interest me, I *do* talk to strangers. From him, ever so diplomatically, I tried to elicit some hint of personal explanation. Why had he come that long, hot, dry stretch to Jailhouse Ruin? What was the attraction?

He couldn't or wouldn't say.

Both, I thought, being himself unsure why he had, except that he wanted to. Equally unsure, perhaps, why he preferred not explaining—assuming that he could. Before beginning the long hike back, he did aim that telephoto at those sun-and-moon pictographs hovering on the cliff just above the ruin. In fact, only a long lens can do their spooky, vaguely menacing images justice. He and his wife inspected the ruin. They had paused, as everyone does, over the corncobs, the potsherds, the half-shattered partitions of wattle-and-daub that implied . . . what?

As the pair began heading back, I asked about pools or seeps they might've seen on their route down. To my surprise, I learned that he and his wife were neither "pumping" nor "treating"; instead, they'd less than a quart to do them that long journey back. Dehydration guaranteed. With a build like his, he could've carried a literal gallon, no problem. Naturally when, in offering some of my water, I assured him I could filter plenty more from a spring not far away, he said, "Thanks all the same. What we've got'll do us till our truck." Male pride, of course. I should've known.

Four years later, I'm still wondering how thirsty he and his wife had become during their return. Any opinions on their water supply she kept to herself in my hearing. More tantalizing, however, has been my guess as to what allure in Anasazi culture had drawn them there. Mum though he was, I admired him then, and still do, just as I take off my hat to any mate, male or female, who says, "Sure, I'll come along." They had stirred their shanks, gone to see for themselves. So the couple at Jailhouse Ruin linger in memory, ruin-bibbers like me.

ꕢ

Roving Anasazi sites scattered among time's mesas and canyons of the Southwest, I've seen other people aplenty. They pore over the roofless, tumbledown kivas, aim cameras at the wattle-and-daub walls, hover above the mosaic of potsherd assortments that others before them have respectfully laid out upon fallen cliff hunks. In breeze dry as the sandstone it erodes, they inspect the juniper roof-traves still in place, take close-ups of rock art while heat comes off that rock like furnace breath. They traipse and ponder and thirst, straggling from fragment to fragment, mumbling to themselves or each other. They endure the midges and gnats, infinitely small, infinitely many, infernally pestiferous. They teeter and clamber, risking their hides. At first they understand no more of archaeology than a mole does of stars, but out of growing curiosity about the past and its people, they pick up smatterings. If in the most discreet terms imaginable, you ask, "Why?" you may not get much of an answer. Most simply stare back at you. Such words as they find amount more often than not to a spoken shrug: "Oh, it's a sort of a hobby" or "Well . . . because."

This state of inarticulate passion isn't limited to broad-shouldered males long on lenses and short on water. For many a season, until I decided to try sounding the bottom of that mystery, it had extended to me, right along with all those others.

Ultimately, of course, "because" is why we do anything, but such an all-purpose word, like a Mexican *piñata,* conceals a dozen different impulses inside it. Among them is a motive that Jailhouse Ruin, more than any I've visited, exemplifies especially well: the pathos of intimacy. True, any human vestige long-abandoned is likely to be tinged with it; however, that feeling is nowhere to be found when, for example, you're in Rome, surrounded by those marble scraps and oddments called the Forum, or by the ruddy cloud of Roman brick called the Baths of Diocletian. Between them you feel the booted strut of legions whose stubby swords and well-drilled maneuvers made the Mediterranean's ancient world pay tribute, literally.

On the other hand, if you wanted a perfect opposite to the Golden House of Nero, Rome's purple silks, and gold coin exacted as protection money; wanted an opposite to the skull racks of the bloodthirsty Aztecs with their encyclopedic cruelty, to the Buddhist stupas of Angkor Wat in Indonesia, or to the Mayan remains at Chichen Itza, so four-square and formally monumental, you couldn't do better than Jailhouse.

For openers, it's so nearly invisible as to hardly be there. Ambling along in good boots over rocky streamed gone dry, flushing doves that whistle as they rise, taking shortcuts all a-prickle with the spiked water of cactus, you wince to consider how little protection the weave of yucca sandals must have given Anasazi feet. You round a bend in the canyon just as you've rounded dozens along the way, seeing the usual ponderosities of Cedar Mesa sandstone, knobbed and domed, some turreted and others rotunda-like, high overhead. Tawny, half-animal forms. Hulking massivities that can't be arrogant, not really, but are, and couldn't care less. Such megatons of them, in petrified colors primevally old and awesome on every side. Then, low under all that, tucked into the merest crevice, you believe maybe you see it.

Perhaps you'd have traipsed right on by, if not for two painted discs looming (that does seem the right word) above what you barely detect as Anasazi masonry. The disks look about two feet wide, chalk white, except where one of them has "eyes"; small circles left unpainted, thus eerily vacuous and staring right at you. Like sun ghost and moon ghost. Unsettling, yet you prefer not to admit it. What motives impelled the prehistoric hand that brushed their whiteness onto that cliff? Invocation of helpful or guardian spirits? Were sun and moon a male/female pairing for them as for us? Floating there, so as to ward off whatever?

Close up, the "jail" aspect proves a misnomer for something far more domestic: peeled sticks set crosswise in adobe to bar the ruin's one surviving window whose span my hat could cover. A turkey pen? Or safehouse for an infant able to crawl? Inside the ruin you see how that window belongs to a natural alcove, rather deep, within which a compartment has been walled off with adobe. Access is by a sort of adobe horse-collar, plumped and rounded into an opening some two feet high by two feet wide. A child-proof gate fitted to its inside entrance could have kept a toddler, or turkeys, corralled and out of trouble while the grown-ups did whatever needed doing. Like so many Anasazi homes, it requires a bit of climbing to reach; a small child unrestrained could easily come to grief.

Opposite that alcove, across a circular "living room" hardly ten feet wide, sits another enclosure, this one thinly walled by wattle-and-daub, with a horse-collar "door" matching the other. Somehow it suggests "bedroom," though we know they used reed mats, not beds. Maybe right there that nameless woman and man curled up, copulated, slept. Maybe there they dreamed they were happy. And, waking, maybe they were. Every least detail of their cozy set-up implies a life, not just an existence: the good-size corncobs, the sacred handprints on their low, smoke-blackened ceilings, the well-formed sherds scattered about, the impressive snugness of their cave's layout. Plus an endearing touch more.

Sandstone projections within their cave being bumpy or askew, upon one of them the woman (surely it was she) had fashioned herself a quite practical "shelf" by overcoming slant with a buildup of adobe some sixteen inches long. She had laid it, tamped it down, and had thereby leveled herself a neat surface for, or so I like to suppose, her kitchen utensils. It was any kitchen shelf in the world, apt for placing ladles, teeny pots of pepper grass, or salt, or wild mustard, or juniper ash—all known to have been Anasazi seasonings. In that minor grace note of convenience, the couple I had met there might have caught sight of themselves, content at having everything so handy. They might have almost remembered living here ages ago: setting a clay pot on embers, stirring the rabbit stew, hearing the distant scream of a peregrine falcon as it returns to its aerie across the way, and like the falcon, being pleased with the outlook from their own perch—a wide, southeasterly stretch in this spirit-filled canyon, over whose rim the morning sun rises.

Even today the agreeable openness seems to explain why that Anasazi farmer climbed to and fro innumerable times: up here, then back down to the spring, toting jar upon jar of water, basket upon basketful of clay, so as to plaster over these wattle-and-daub partitions.

I also see him in his sandy field, drilling deep with his planting stick, then dropping seed kernels into each hole. I see his equally hard-working mate stooped low, watering every one of their corn plants as carefully as if it were a child. The two of them making a go of it.

Had they, in fact, any children? One, maybe, or a couple? Even three? Not likely. Sharing quarters *so* snug with a third child would have surely moved them on. Maybe one did. Moved them for reasons like our own: more room, better chances, which in their case might have been a slightly more arable bean patch, a few extra hills of corn.

In short, the pleasure of pathos at Jailhouse Ruin arises from our all but eye-witnessing an intimacy long gone, of spaces still warmly human, though emptied these eight, nine hundred years. Unlike Italy's Etruscans, who survive only in tombs and funerary urns, the vanished inhabitants here survive in cups, pots, sandals, handprints of ancient routines real and humble as our own. Somehow, as the bodies they belonged to step forth from dust, then back again into dust, there's an oddly satisfying peace in thereby touching ourselves across so great a distance, gently consenting, one day, to become that man and that woman.

⑥

So much for ruin on an intimate scale. While a single aspect of any given Anasazi site may dominate our awareness, the satisfaction from exploring such tangible relics is far more complex than most of us wannabe Anasazi are aware. Also among its elements is one we might call the pleasure of surmise.

Jailhouse invites us to guesswork that *creates* what's missing. Facing what has survived, we supply what hasn't and thereby throw time into reverse, building up in imagination what's fallen away from crumbled walls. Our mind's eye sets about patching holes in adobe partition, restores broken pots to their likely places, and summons even the people who used them. Their naked little kids too, if we're inclined. We may hear far off the voices of neighbors (one of them chanting, possibly?) as his stone hoe rises and falls. Why not?

Mightn't we hear, too, just down the canyon, a run of notes from someone's wooden flute? If from the silence that makes itself at home in such long-abandoned places, those imagined notes should tell us we're getting a bit fanciful, we could ask ourselves, "What people ever lived without music?"

Whereas in Bullet Canyon the scale of surmisal is quite limited, among the Great Houses and Great Kivas of Chaco Canyon its scope expands to a challenge. While daydreaming either there or in Colorado, beside the Great Kiva at Lowry, or at the mysterious ruin of Chimney Rock, the pleasure of surmise is complicated further. As the mind's eye restores what those structures *were,* our bodily eyesight scans what they've *become.* In gazing through and beyond what now *is* into what *was,* we effect a complex double exposure of the ruin.

And more. Among the most imposing of Anasazi structures, such as the restored Great Kiva at Aztec, New Mexico, or the many hundreds of excavated but unrestored rooms at Yellow Jacket, Colorado, there is also the factor of respect mounting to awe as we picture the effort. Archaeologist W. James Judge once estimated that 215,000 beams were carried into Chaco Canyon, many from quite a distance. Some trunks, lugged from sixty miles away, were more than two feet thick and proportionately long, to say nothing of prodigious heaps of stone quarried or gathered in Chaco's immediate area. First-time visitors to that canyon's famous Great House called Pueblo Bonito often fall silent, realizing what had been built by so relatively few, with so little, so long since.

No steel, no glass, no concrete. For mortar, mud. For machinery, human muscle and bone. Gazing on the relics of such effort, carried out over centuries, aware what impressive feats of organization they required, aware they'd been planned and seen through without writing, we enjoy the humility our admiration implies.

௫

The dark side of visiting ruins, however, is morbidity. Not a skull-and-crossbones kind of *memento mori*. Instead, the strange pleasure in eye-witnessing, as it were, our own annihilation.

Far west of Chaco, amid the heft of dunes and low hills, near a Great House called Kin Bineola (Navajo for "place of the swirling winds"), I looked at its high walls and tried, as I had often done, to account for their fastidious masonry. Had ritual scrupulosity of some sort impelled the builders? Narrow blades of shale in their thousands had been patiently, accurately fitted to each other, then plastered over by adobe. I admired their craftsmanship even while feeling a morbid pleasure in what time has overthrown.

Terrain in that area yields building material whose color, unlike Chaco's palominos and tans, verges on a somber, almost shadowy red. The sun that June morning had been warm, not torrid. And because Kin Bineola is rarely visited, I had very much relished having the place to myself.

I remember the hush, my own wordless disturbing of grasses, thistles, while focusing a wide-angle lens on those beautifully desolate walls; and clearly recall how cautiously I moved there, owing to an abiding hunch that I just might be sharing Kin Bineola with a rattler or two. Yet even as I admired thick, rubble-core walls so meticulously veneered by gone hands, and looked into room upon room built up by their stonework, my delight arose equally from their slow stone-by-stone dilapidation: rubble that summarized winds, rainy skies of almost a millennium.

Lustrous and graceful on their long stems, stands of "needle-and-thread grass" had nodded wordlessly to each other as, with shadscale bushes and a few low puffs of greasewood, they continued their slow repossession of the place. Abundant thistles stood tall in rooms long roofless, and maybe it was they that brought to mind something one Thomas Whately had written. He, an eighteenth-century Englishman, had also pondered the melancholy pleasure in seeing grand endeavors overgrown by plant life: "No circumstance," he wrote, "so forcibly marks the desolation of a spot once inhabited, as the prevalence of Nature over it." To which he added a Latin phrase, *Jam seges est ubi Troja fuit,* translatable as a couplet: "Where Troy's walls and towers rose / A level field of wheat now grows."

Odd, on a fine summer's morning, to let your own living hand touch the futility of all human effort, the sure destruction of every mortal thing, and yet feel no sadness. But we rational animals are indeed mixed creatures. Even as we take a sort of pleasure in facing our future made visible, we prefer not to admit it.

A cynic might put that more bluntly: "Your satisfaction in ruin— if you *dare* be honest about it—arises from malice. Since you know someday you'll die, you're secretly pleased at seeing how everything and everybody else will, too."

Assuredly, there's some consolation in knowing, as mortals, we've plenty of company, and I suppose consolation *is* remotely like pleasure. But I'm certain our yen for exploring plazas, kivas, and storerooms left by the Anasazi feels much, much warmer and closer than any long-distance, retroactive spite. There's incomparably more satisfaction in imagining a village's chattery men, its women gathering clay, mixing adobe; in picturing them as they lay well-chosen stones, so as to be sure that a doorway—one of the dozens at Kin Bineola, for example—rises four-square and plumb; more satisfaction, I'd say, than in feasting our eyes on their skeletons. We're made that way as well: to love only what dies.

ᕫ

To some extent, the compassion excited in us by ruination masks the pleasures of escapism, a sort of wishful transcendence. Anasazi vestiges not only evoke a pleasurable Elsewhere; they also send us, by a motion of our souls, *toward* another space whose lives and times, by comparison, feel contentedly sane. Visiting their tumble-down hamlets near coyote-colored mesas, picking our next move amid rattler-colored rocks, we enjoy getting carried away, into their wilder, more wide-open world, under skies they presumed to be endless as the most perfect of circles.

By contrast, our present atmosphere is jet-streaked and be-smogged. Our jobs often leave us feeling we're being bustled along a treadmill while wearing a straitjacket. Meanwhile, back home, very little in daily use is either homegrown or handmade, and we live in a house, chances are, whose mortgage we can only hope we'll survive.

Small wonder we feel deeply the appeal of settlements where raw materials were free for the gathering, where each family had every skill necessary to shape them. When bowls, cups, pots were required, the women knew arroyos in which the best clay was to be found, knew how to knead it, build each form out of coils, smooth their inner and outer walls; knew from their mothers how to slip and paint each design, then how best to harden that ware with fire. Similarly, the men knew how to prepare a field for corn, beans, or squash, understood how deep each must be planted, how to keep ravens from the seed, and rabbits from nibbling the shoots; knew how to lay roof-traves over house walls, then put down reed matting and top it with clay tamped solid; knew how to weave turkey-feather robes, rabbit-fur jackets; how to plait yucca leaves into sandals, or how with a back-loom to weave fine cotton fabrics.

Primitive? Yes, but wouldn't it feel good to regress, to live among townsfolk where nobody has a job? Where instead of jobs, everybody has a life, and every life a clear purpose? Through those homemade little villages now so sun-and-moon bitten—whose people lived a togetherness we'll never have and maybe couldn't stand, except in imagination—we momentarily slip into the simpler patterns of their missing lives.

Lives we ourselves once lived, now forgotten? That feeling is strong among Anasazi rooms, as pastimes from childhood half awaken: turning out mud pies, shaping cups from mud; building "forts" and "clubhouses" from scrap lumber, cartons, fallen branches, any old thing we kids could lay hands on; stringing cord to a willow bow that actually shot twig "arrows" we didn't yet know how to feather; stacking "pretend" campfires with green sticks set like a tepee over grass handfuls.

I suspect that Anasazi kivas, for instance, with their roof-hole and ladder—down which we descend into dramatic shadow and exclusivity—take us back to childhood unaware, back to summers of tribal rites shared by the neighborhood's other make-believe Indians. So partly the transcendence promoted by such ruins sends us pleasantly back to those early years of fun and games—and grace.

Partly. Leading "the inner child" down into that kiva, our adult selves enter *at the same time* something wider, more profound: a sort of outlying kinship.

The long-gone are easy to love. Because they've taken their bad habits and body stink, their reeking piles of nightsoil, rotten garbage, turkey droppings, and fly swarms with them; because their abodes are fouled now by nothing more noxious than packrats, we can press their dear, prehistoric absences to our bosoms. Regardless of whether that kinship's a fantasy, our pleasure in it is real, is liberating—an escape from self, the "me." From the incessantly mumbling, grumbling, scheming, blithering first-person singular. It's a brief but soothing release. Strictly speaking, of course, we know that our best-informed guesses about the New World's stone-age mind may leave us on the outside looking out, not in. Trying to see things as the Anasazi saw them may be like drinking the waters of a mirage.

᧖

Perhaps our most gratifying pleasure in Southwestern ruins is finding them. To foil pothunters and vandals, the U.S. Geological Survey no longer maps the positions of significant relics not already common knowledge. But the inventory is still in progress. So, just as my man at Jailhouse had done along the trail, you keep an eye out. It's like prospecting, or like being on the prowl after someone, looking for "sign."

And having learned Anasazi requirements, you may get to be rather good at it, knowing your binoculars needn't scan any north-facing cliff, because all dwellings had a southeasterly outlook so as to be "passive solar" during months of low sun, with overhang enough for shade when the sun climbs high overhead. And had to have access to water, naturally. Access to planted fields. Defensible position, depending on what nomadic marauders of, say, a thousand years back had been up to.

Among Anasazi buffs, "keeping an eye out" becomes so ingrained you must will *not* to do it.

Rather, you can try. I've never succeeded longer than ten minutes at a stretch. With my son Nick I once did fifteen miles southward down Fish Creek Canyon in southern Utah and then back north up Owl Creek Canyon, trying to quit looking. When the trail allowed my eyes to glance upward along the rim, they did so without asking permission. Our trip had aimed at enjoying the canyons themselves: the May blossoms of penstemon and mariposa lily, the collared lizards, the hummingbirds, the hawks, the odd badger galumphing along. Repeatedly, however, like a drying-out lush who keeps trying not to recall the aroma of bourbon, I had to pull my eyes back from scanning for sites just below the high rims right and left of us: sites convenient for farming up there on the plateau. Despite trying not to, I spotted a ruin, then another. Or were they? Four hundred feet up and much too vertical for any casual look-see, they remained hypothetical.

Because Anasazi masonry can be a perfect match with broken strata occurring naturally in canyon walls, you spot dozens of "ruins" geology put there, never inhabited by any but fossil sea worms or crinoids, if at all. Even in places like Grand Gulch, happy hunting ground for ruin-bibbers, with habitations encaved near the base of cliff walls, they're still slightly above canyon floor, often hidden by cottonwoods grown thick since abandonment. So legs already trail weary may pass a long day scrambling only twenty feet up, but *many* times, boots backsliding in sandy shale, then bushwhack through yet more leafy branches to discover nothing. Or find near charcoal and sherds a small adobe shelter with, just above it, handprints! A pair of them: left hand, right hand. Their whole story, a pigment's dark red pressed onto that shallow cave's sandstone. Under such influences, you don't feel driven, you feel drawn.

ᔕ

Pompeii's frescoed centaurs or satyrs; a well-muscled, lyre-strumming Orpheus; winsome partridges and hares nibbling wide-eyed among grape vines—all are expressions of a culture where painting had long since become a specialized profession. But Rome's sophisticated imagery resides in brain spaces very different from where Anasazi folk art is received.

On top on that, there's the Euro-machinery of mass tourism. Our approaches to Mediterranean antiquities have been so channeled, so surrounded and programmed—first by written histories, by coffee-table books, by posters, then by travel brochures—that a sightseer reaching *even* the wonderful Greek temples in Sicily or Egypt's pharaonic temple at Luxor may feel like raw material in a factory process, "seeing" mostly what he's read or been told.

It's utterly different when handprints suddenly float up before you, alone in a Southwestern canyon: no guidebook, no ballyhoo. No placard set alongside, explaining. Because one size fits all, such hands become yours easy as breathing.

Then there's the fact that, unlike those in Europe, a goodly portion of Southwestern antiquities lie open to anyone caring to explore them. Sites long known but unpillaged in Navajo territory

have been spared by Navajo fear of spirits, as if the dead were conta-
gious. Like everything else among traditional peoples, that fear has
been modified by the twentieth century but hasn't vanished.

At the mouth of Arizona's Tsegi Canyon, a Navajo woman working for the Park Service put a human face on the death-dread I'd
known only from books. She was young, twenty-five or so. I had
asked her to show me round Betatakin Ruin, but her first remark
was an apology for her deep blue T-shirt and jeans. "It's because I'm
new," she said. "I just got hired three weeks ago. My Park Service
uniform hasn't come yet."

"What's your Navajo name?" I asked.

"Well, it would be, in English . . . like Delight Laughter."

That made me grin, of course, all the more because her round,
brown face wore a grave expression. When I asked how the new job
suited her, she grew more serious yet.

"My grandmother didn't want me to take this job. She said, 'You
shouldn't go near those places. They should be left alone. You
shouldn't be there. You shouldn't be taking people to them.'"

Among traditional Navajo that wariness still operates, but dry
climate is the main preservative. It has kept artifacts, and even bodies, deceptively fresh; for example, the Nevada mummy called
"Spirit Cave man" had been thought 2,000 years old until recent im-
provements in radiocarbon dating showed him 7,400 years *older*.
Nearly ten millennia dead! Yet with him were bits of cloth impressively woven.

To archaeology's vexed question—"Who owns the past?"—the
pothunter's response is, "It's mine—for the ransacking!" A vandal
attitude, that, and crude as loot. Still, a hiker toward Yapashi or the
Stone Lions shrine remains largely on his own best archaeological
behavior. Little is roped off, no terminally bored custodian tells you
to stand farther back. No guide avid for gratuities runs robotically
through a spiel for his busload of tour-packaged and much-rumpled
pilgrims. At Wupatki you're left to yourself, looking, thinking,

breathing quietly amid Anasazi stones so red as to seem quarried from leftover sunset. All the Southwest is like that: a vast open-air museum where *you* are both guide and guard. Laws protect every such site, of course, but when alone there, abiding by them is between you and your conscience. And what delight *would* you take in ruins if you lacked one?

ⓢ

Southwestern light and color and air. Withholding emphasis on them isn't quite like saving the best for last, though almost. When it comes to proto-Pueblos like the Anasazi, the who without the where becomes unimaginable, so fused was their culture with the high deserts whose mysteries they lived in and by means of. Thus that setting gives rise to what I might whimsically label "the pleasures of where."

Rain's feast-or-famine habits in the Southwest lean toward the famine side so visibly that, without asking, you *know* precipitation's annual average. Stunted ambitions of four-winged saltbush, the considerable distance between junipers, the underprivileged look of yucca clumps, Mormon tea, all tell the same story: "Rain? Not nearly enough." So do the more impressive ruins. You might say it was ghost rain that emptied Chaco Canyon's layout of Great Houses.

Aridity has, however, kept prehistory so incomparably well that for more than a century now the high deserts across our interior West have trained generations of American archaeologists.

Nowhere on Earth, not even Greece and Egypt, has seen more students learn how to study the tangible past. Tree-ring dating, dating by radioactivity, spectrographic analysis of turquoise, looking backward at ecological changes as revealed by packrat middens, genetic "fingerprinting" in various strains of maize—all have been brought to bear on prehistory of the Southwest. Understanding their contributions toward our picture of this or that ruin is, I admit, a *kind* of pleasure. A "higher" kind, in theory, because intellectual. Yet as pleasure it's pretty thin stuff when, for example, I think of Keet Seel, and of the catch put in my breath by something I saw there: the heat-shadows of four corn cakes, left on an Anasazi cookstone centuries before Columbus.

ဪ

Just as hues in light's actual spectrum change so invisibly that the eye can't say precisely where yellow turns orange or orange blurs into hot red, who's to say where pathos of intimacy modulates to our delight in surmising the look of a ruin when newly built and teeming with people? Where morbidity and escapist delight seem aspects of each other, how can we tell which is dominant in any given moment? Is it possible to keep an imagined past unpenetrated by its ruinous present? While letting time and fate stare us square in the eye, as adobe-mortared stone tells our fortunes, we quietly accept what their dilapidation portends: our own fathomless oblivion.

But only sooner or later. Only someday. Even as we stare into death's gaping maw, our heart's blood, warm and sassy, enjoys thumbing its nose at The Inevitable. Meanwhile we enter those same ruins at, say, El Morro in northwestern New Mexico, or Canyon de Chelly in Arizona, or Edge of the Cedars in Utah, as if into a sort of "noble savage" Elsewhere, letting Anasazi enigmas implicit at Chaco or Chimney Rock become a tangible transcendence: a unity, however rude, of dwellings, tools, and clothes handmade by the fellow humans who used them.

Strange pleasure, stepping again and again from this world into an Anasazi one from which such an attunement disappeared forever. Akin to that nostalgic transcendence may be our unconscious return, through Anasazi doorways, to the lost summers of childhood, before our lives split into "home" and "job," often miles apart.

Childlike, too, the questing, the discovery, the keeping eyes peeled for Anasazi rudiments, like salty old codgers on the lookout for a rich vein. But along mesa trails and canyons of the Southwest, prehistoric relics are a far likelier discovery than gold-bearing ore. At Texas Canyon in Utah I recall scanning all afternoon for peregrine falcons and, having spotted none, felt I'd saved the day by finding a ruin somewhat rare because its big beams, still intact, hadn't been spied out and burnt up for firewood by nineteenth-century sheepherders.

Although rain-skimpy skies over the Colorado Plateau have taken better care of the past than we have, scattered across that plateau are mud-mortared walls, poignantly fragile but still *there;* juniper roof-traves; handprints whose ruddy pigment is a pulverized hematite that eight hundred, a thousand, and more than a thousand years haven't granulated away. Those half-miraculous preservations aren't the least of one's pleasures in ruin. Nor that high desert's incomparable space. Nor toward sundown, despite killer suns of midafternoon, its inner distances speaking in tongues of light and shadow.

As for a New Mexico, Arizona, or Utah evening, your mood there can invest time's barest necessities with an allure so narcotic you feel on the verge of understanding things no one will ever understand.

In fact, a June evening near my tent on the rim of Dark Canyon virtually did that. Red rock, creamy cloud, blue sky. Desert stillness like some wordless dream-voice telling a sleeper who he really is. Then low sun through manzanita foliage and curl-leaf mahogany slowly made their leaves translucent, while smearing that entire bush-stippled rim in green-gold. I was just standing there, admiring, when my own voice surprised me by murmuring aloud and to no one, "I'm home." Two words. Only those.

I've a hunch they may suggest yet another pleasure in Southwestern ruination. Through Anasazi vestiges, we perhaps pay our respects to what's missing in us, thus honoring those ancient ones (a bit ruefully?) as a people able to live out lives undivided from themselves. Lives we need their help even to imagine.

Ravens at Deadhorse Canyon

"Those who are wise love water." Whatever China's ancient sage Chuang Tzu may have meant by that, I'm unsure, but surely he had noticed water's placidity and flow inducing thoughtful moods in minds other than his own.

At times a solo canoe trip can feel like one long, fluent meditation. Just hours ago, while paddling downstream on Utah's Green River, I rounded a gooseneck bend called Turk's Head and caught sight of John Wesley Powell's "Buttes of the Cross." For his sake, as well as for themselves, I loved their lofty, otherworldly silhouettes: monumental forms of russet sandstone conspicuously separated from plateau-size buttes by such gods as inhabit the word "erosion." In contrast, the Anasazi ruins at Turk's Head had been disappointing, one or two small granaries, so Powell associations now help compensate, even if from my camp I get only a glimpse of one butte's cliff.

I like having that glimpse, less for amusement at the Powell era's bible-thumping taste in place names than for him, a man I admire extravagantly. Somehow, gazing on Green River sights *he* had seen back in 1869 brings him nearer.

With a widening spiral the raven pair high to my left have been riding their thermal like the simplest uplift in the world, a good two thousand feet in less than two minutes. As they tilt and soar, still climbing, their outstretched wings catch occasional glints off an evening sun that they seem—so gracefully, lazily—to have risen well above. I've the impression these may enjoy the cool-down of evening just as I do, though not in my own species' day-dream way. In flight, rather; as if they love making what's impossible for us look supremely easy, and without even knowing they do it.

My scientific side, such as it is, reminds me that "know" is misused on ravens. Meanwhile, my eyes tell me it isn't. They tell me these ravens know they can fly, despite their not knowing they know it. Watching their side-by-side upward circling, I begin, as usual when pondering this particular aspect of raven behavior, to back away from our derisive phrase "bird brain." High, *way* high overhead, this pair of corvids give every appearance of flying for the pure pleasure of wings.

Are they mates? They must be. Their motions match each other in cruising maneuvers that don't quite coincide, which seems more "human" somehow, by implying that each has a certain leeway and is therefore more truly a mate, not a mechanism—not a feathered echo of traits in evolution's ongoing agenda.

With an easy sweep of wing one now veers off, solo. Is my "mate theory" about to be disproven? The second raven delays as if to keep me in suspense, then with a similar wing-sweep follows. Soon *it* becomes leader, heading off on a gentle if independent swerve, which within a quarter-minute or so its mate imitates. For a full half-minute they glide alongside each other, wavering, turning, almost as one. How companionable they seem! Like any well-agreed human couple out for an evening stroll, taking the air together.

In another hour and a half the sun will have set, but till then, taking the air isn't a bad idea. If only I could. I had thought the Green River might be cool as its name, but this afternoon the tiny "Weather Bob" thermometer attached to my pack's black fabric said 120°F—high as its tiny red column can go. I thought it broken. True, that was in direct sun, but it was also midstream, aboard my canoe! Now, almost sundown in my shaded campsite, it still reads

94°F, even as hot gusts through nearby cottonwoods set the fat leaves clacking ironically like rain.

ᕲ

A decade ago, and two hundred miles south of my present camp, far down in the Grand Canyon (another Powell passage), I had once sat for hours on a sandstone ledge doing what I'm doing right now: absolutely nothing. Not coincidentally, it was at this same sundown time of evening, when a different kind of raven startled me with a revelation like an intimate disclosure.

Fahrenheits of midafternoon had felt like somebody ironing my clothes while I was still in them. Then, as Arizona's big bullroarer of a sun slowly lowered toward eclipse by the canyon's north rim, my ledge's overlook had turned with the Earth into merciful shade. Like a war orphan finally reaching a neutral zone, at last I could breathe, could open to the Inner Canyon's blue-golds of distance, along with its nearer rust-red panoramas. Unforgettable effects, as everyone knows. But it was a lone raven alighting on my ledge that made the evening special.

It had ridden an updraft from far below, then expertly fluffed down twelve feet away, where it perched at the lip of a pothole, the better to sip leftover rain. A small raven it was, tossing its head back after each beakful as if to gargle, then dipping again for another fill.

Between sips the bird cocked its head at angles, now this way, now that, in the wary habit of survival. A few minutes earlier, from one of the ledge's larger basins of rain, I myself had not only drunk, but with my bandanna and Dr. Bronner's biodegradable soap, had managed a rather sketchy stand-up bath.

So, sun gone down, thirst quenched, there we sat, quietly together. Maybe the raven's afternoon had been as sun-stunned as mine. Welcome currents of updraft flowed past us, tousling my hair, ruffling the raven's neck feathers. Yet as they lightly lifted in breeze, then settled, then again lifted, my eyes widened. The neck's under-feathers weren't black but white—cloud white, white as any Paraclete! And as each wafting updraft subsided, the neck feathers settled down to being again coal-black, like those of any other raven. It seemed I was being let in on something, a confidence, almost an intimacy.

I began feeling humiliation to match my surprise. Despite half a lifetime shared with Colorado ravens, had I been some kind of blind fool? How could the entire species have kept this from me till now? If *all* their necks were so feathered—outwardly raven but inwardly white as doves—how could I possibly have failed to notice?

The embarrassed mood soon passed. A recollection from one of my field guides made me grin at my own silliness as the term "white-necked raven" came to mind. So I hadn't "failed to notice," hadn't been duped. This smallish fellow was merely one of that white-necked species, *Corvus cryptoleucus*; my first ever, outside of books. First and last, as it happens, because I've yet to see another. They're common enough, as I've since learned, though the Grand Canyon does lie somewhat north of their usual range.

We continued eyeing each other for several minutes. Every now and again, as those neck feathers tousled, revealing the whiteness I'd found such a surprise, my earlier sense of being *confided in* had returned. The raven—by merely resting there, by agreeing to share that ledge with me, by slaking his thirst from the same rain, by allowing breeze to give away his secret—had closed the rift our all-too-human vanity puts between us and fellow animals. Sooner or later each of us would die, though only one of us knew it. No matter. In addition to heat fatigue and thirst, we had life, and the evening, and our canyon ledge in common. There we sat, wordless, content not to stir.

Questing toward some imagined Grand Happiness, we find it rarely if ever; meanwhile, a few blessed moments find us. They're not anything we'd know how to look for. Besides, that's not how it works. The blessed moments aren't targetable. They just happen. Years later, merely recollecting them can summon us back to our best selves, but only if when they come, we're not too busy to see them for what they are. A lone *Corvus cryptoleucus* bestowed one of mine. A convergence of two lives without the least impulse to be anywhere or anything else.

ⓢ

Miles to the southeast, far beyond the huge Utah buttes that Powell named, a purplish few rain clouds are just now pouring their heat-relief soundlessly down, letting their waters go at the speed of gravity, which distance transforms to slow motion, and to the rain sashes that Pueblo dancers wear imitations of. Typical of most showers on the Colorado Plateau, its wetness isn't hitting anything but air. It's virga, instead, the ghost rain that dries up as it falls. But that's Utah June. And July. And mostly year-round here. Except for August.

August will, or should, bring the "rainy season." Not very, of course. Even by August this litter of cottonwood twigs scattered round my teal-blue tent would still be brittle as crackers, but I expect the streambed of Deadhorse Canyon would no longer be, as now, dry cobbles and powdery sand. Yet August is rainy as Utah's red-rock country ever gets; eight annual inches in some parts, little as four in others. Small wonder that ceremonies of desert-dwelling Indians from prehistoric through historic have stayed focused on rain—which is to say, on life: the life coming down from the sky. This same sky my raven pair seem so to delight in.

Indians gave animals credit for wisdom surpassing that of humans: serpents most of all because so inscrutable, but badgers, too, honey ants, tumblebugs, magpies and piñon jays; and wolf spiders and desert bighorn sheep, black bears and beetles, antelope—the whole arkful. As forerunners of the animal-sensitive Pueblos, surely the Anasazi felt so, too. Ironically, even while we smile at Indian naivete about animal "wisdom," our past half-century has finally *begun* awakening to truths animals can teach us about ourselves.

To suppose that these ravens, now so specklike high overhead, "enjoy" their power of flight is, of course, guesswork on my part. For years, despite watching dozens of raven pairs "take the evening air" in that same playful way—gliding now together, now sidling apart, one above then below the other—I've resisted upgrading it to more than a projective error: lending some "me" to "them." Animals don't "think," however much we may think they seem to. Whatever they appear to be up to at any given moment, their aim is either food or sex, which comes down to simply passing on genes.

That's what the animal scientists tell us, and I've entire faith in them. Almost. This evening, however, camped near the mouth of a canyon called Deadhorse, the raven pair I've been watching—who couldn't care less what I do or do not believe—tell me that sometimes things *are* what they seem. And tell me to believe what I'm seeing.

Song Dog

A New Mexican morning, 5:32 A.M. But perhaps there won't be a visible sunrise, given this reef of cloud low to my northeastern horizon. Too thick, maybe, for the solar sphere to break through. Meanwhile, coyotes are calling with an insistence that puzzles me, and closer than those I often hear this early. Usually they sound like weanlings or pups demanding to know—via yowls, yelps, howls, and sustained yips—just where their next meal is coming from, and *when*. Presumably Mom or Pop Coyote or both have long since gone out on the prowl, sniffing summer grasses for field mice.

But this morning, under a soft, cumulus-bottomed overcast, I rather enjoy the effect of a dawn sky muted as twilight. Is that why those coyotes sound so much nearer? Signaling each other, working out the game plan? Omnivores hatching some meat-eating scheme?

What a contrast their hullabaloo makes with the meadowlark tip-topping a ponderosa pine just to my left. His call repeats its run: a clear, lilting, territorial warble. Then again. Yet again. And each time, from somewhere east in the meadow, comes another meadow-lark's counterclaim of reply.

Because I'm not far from Jemez Springs and the Jemez Pueblo, it occurs to me that those Pueblo ancestors, the Anasazi, never petro-glyphed coyotes; or, more accurately, I should say, if they did peck that critter's image onto stone, I've not seen it. Desert bighorn sheep, yes, I've seen hundreds of those petroglyphs, and deer, and dancers with deer heads. In historical times, one of the vilest insults a Pueblo could hurl at your head was "Coyote!" so maybe coyote imagery lacked whatever sanction petroglyphics had to have.

On the other hand, Coyote commanded more than contempt among Pueblos, and among Native Americans generally, owing to his enduring cleverness and persistence. No scheme proved too outrageous for at least a try, once it entered his conniving brain— no matter how many times other crazy ambitions had landed him in a cactus patch or skinned alive. Coyote story-lore is so widespread among Indians that his yapping and crooning *had* to be an everyday sound among the Anasazi as well. Small wonder one of his Indian names is "Song Dog."

Considerably downslope from me, nearer that coyote yowling, a couple of grazing mule deer have taken an interest. Their heads come up, their ears swivel toward the high, tenor-like notes sustained by one coyote in particular. Soon those two deer are joined by a third. The three of them stand alert, poised, focused, as if asking each other, "Is this likely to get serious?" That, too, is unusual. I've seen a herd of fifteen or so mule deer completely ignore the lone coyote trotting toward, then right through, then past them without so much as one deer getting skittish or letting more than a sidelong glance interrupt its browse.

This morning, despite signs of anxiety in those three does, nothing happens. The coyote cantata doesn't even dwindle away with their usual straggle of casual or petulant yelps. Just stops. As if somebody had pulled the plug. Which leaves me and maybe the deer wondering, "What was *that* all about?"

Whatever it may have been, it certainly renewed my sense of how well Coyote's trickster reputation accords with his voice. Millions of youngsters who've never heard any but a TV coyote can give a coyote howl—though it may come out sounding like their dog's memory of having once been a wolf. But how many kids or grownups know by ear the coyote's full repertoire of yips, screeches, and long-sustained, ululating howls? Those latter are indeed famously mournful. Overhearing one from a half-mile off, I stop in my tracks, listening. As that beginning low-throated call rises in pitch, its despair sounds so total I almost *see* the uplifted snout twisting, distorting, and the creature's blond throat fur pulse with the climactic, eerie vibrato.

What begins as a coyote solo is sometimes followed by the whole pack's tumbling cascade of yelps, as if somebody in a bar for manic drunks had suddenly announced free drinks. Yet I suspect it's a sound as ancient as almost any in the animal world. Among his repertoire of disguises and existences, Coyote is in a sense still Anasazi—invisible even when seen—because often you don't realize he's there. Just as cliff dwellings can be indistinguishable from the sandstone crevice into which they were built, coyote pelage seems chameleon-hued to match his surroundings; desert dust, the gray-green of sage or of lichened rock, the blond of sandstone, or the burlap tinge of winter grasses. Without snow to set him off, his motion's the only thing your eye can pick up. Otherwise he's part of the scenery. At two hundred yards I've spotted coyotes sitting in full view on a mesa slope, but only by the very slight giveaway of their lighter-colored throat fur as the snout tilted upward in sustaining the howl that revealed it.

Coyote song, too, is most assuredly "an ancient one." With ears that might as well be Anasazi ears, we hear the barks and yelps they heard, the same notes that *begin* shrill, rising fast to a note higher yet, piercingly so. Then a long pause. After which Coyote's throat may go low, low as bloodhounds, or may sound as if he'd suddenly slipped out of his fur into feathers, with voice so like a rooster's crowing that any first-time listener might well be fooled, especially if right around daybreak. How his song carries! And carries within it many a lonely mile.

Coyote howls most movingly, though, in cold too bone-numbing for even his cleverness to feel anything but miserable, in a winter world he never made and maybe wants out of. Snow already too knee-deep for hunting, with more in the air heading down, his song then darkens to a dirge; spookily human, funereal. Out around nightfall, trudging toward home through that snow, I've often stopped in my tracks and stood still while all my gone ancestors listened with me, and answered, "Yes, we understand. We too have been there."

Packrat as Anasazi

They were here first. As cliff dwellers, they could have given the Anasazi lessons, and perhaps did. By building in deep rock crevices well before the Anasazi, or anyone, they dwelt in canyon walls for much the same reasons as impelled the builders at Mesa Verde, Canyon de Chelly, Walnut Canyon, and elsewhere: comfort, shelter, defense.

But the Anasazi cleared out, leaving masonry villages and towers clean empty of life, whereas the packrat has stayed on, adding, as he always had done, new depth and extent to his many-roomed mansions, adding thickness and hardness to their walls, when they had any. And so getting by, or thriving, or undergoing hard times.

This is not the end of his story. Its unfolding continues, still, at Anasazi sites great and small, all of which had been his ages before bipeds arrived there and have long since reverted to him, the original tenant. He has stamina. In those lands of little rain he had learned exemplarily well how to live, what to do, many thousands of years before the first human foot pressed into Southwestern sand or appeared in North America.

If a prehistoric dwelling has survived a half-dozen centuries, we judge it old. Very many of the packrat's have lasted ten times that long. A structure begun six millennia ago? And still in use? That seems more than merely "unlikely." But 6,000 years isn't the half of it. Some of his dwellings date back 20,000 years, and older ones yet at 23,000, 27,000, and so on. The currently earliest of his sites has been radiocarbon dated at 40,000 years prior to our own birthdays. Antiquity like that should make him a Paleo-something, and would, except that he is as busily and numerously our contemporary as ever, even though his houses of greatest age do qualify as Paleomiddens.

Yes, lots of animals amass the piled-up gatherings called middens, but only the packrat's middens have such endurance, many because preserved by a substance called amberat, which, unlike amber, is crystallized urine. Packrats are dedicated, desert-adapted, full-time teetotalers who don't even drink water. Their body fluids depend entirely on vegetation, hence their urine is highly condensed. Like amber, amberat may encase and preserve what otherwise would be dispersed by time's four winds. But whereas amber is rock-solid resin that stays hard whatever the weather, amberat, being "hygroscopic," can in humid conditions sag and soften like January molasses. So fecal pellets, leaves, twigs, rabbit bones—anything the tiny, acquisitive packrat has dragged home for adding to his midden—sooner or later blends in. Along with whatever debris the wind scatters thither, it all consolidates, century by century, into a great, guanolike mass, but with the consistency, as one researcher explains, of asphalt or unfired adobe.

Before I knew about amberat I used to see the stuff, recognizing the rodent pellets within it, but didn't understand what that sticky, honeylike coating was. It did indeed have the look of a syrupy goo, making somewhat understandable the now-famous mistake of some Forty-Niners back in Gold Rush days. Their group had crossed a dried-up lake about sixty miles northwest of Las Vegas, Nevada. Part way into a canyon's narrow secrets they had spied amberat-coated middens, with no idea what they were seeing, except that it looked edible: "We came to a high cliff and in its face were niches or cavities as large as a barrel or larger, and in some of them, we found balls of a glistening substance looking like pieces of variegated candy stuck together." Maybe the resemblance of amberat to honey or syrup improved the taste, because taste it some did: "It was evidently food of some sort, and we found it sweet but sickish, and those who were hungry . . . making a good meal of it, were a little troubled with nausea afterwards."

ॐ

Recently, during an evening walk from my campsite in Utah's Millard Canyon, I grew more and more impressed both with the canyon's rare spaciousness beyond its narrow mouth, and with evidence that almost every third crevice in its beautiful walls of Cedar Mesa sandstone contained packrat architecture. Admittedly, "architecture" stretches the truth almost as far as Millard Canyon is broad and long. Packrat style in housing is less construction than accumulation, accretion. In fact, anyone unfamiliar with packrat habits might mistake their helter-skelter of saltbush twigs, juniper scraps, raven or rabbit bones, and cactus fragments for mere storm-scourings washed down from above. Although on that Millard Canyon evening no packrat nests I saw seemed middens of great age, looking instead like plant rubbish huddled together, I knew that even such loosely assembled dens can also turn out, on inspection, to be surprisingly ancient. Proving that, however, would mean not only taking them apart but also shipping off samples for testing.

Well, if you're a packrat, life is tough enough without having your den destroyed just to ease some hiker's curiosity. Your survival depends on keeping a low profile, about three inches high. Because you're a daytime stay-at-home, chances are your sand-colored fur and long tail haven't evolved as sexual attractions. When night falls, you go forth to feed on or gather what's nearby, and even then you move in those quick dart-and-peek scurries common to rodents. Rarely do you venture far from your hideout—less than a stone's throw, on average. For you, a *long* way from home is eighty or ninety yards. At two-thirds of a pound or thereabouts you'd make a tasty mouthful for coyotes, so among your other incentives in lying low during daylight hours are owls, snakes, hawks, weasels, bears; in short, the usual suspects, against whose meat-eating habits you've developed wide, wide eyes and big ears.

To give your midden some barbed wire, as it were, you may lace it with cactus scraps, but knowing instinctively that a few stickers can't be expected to turn back all who would eat you alive, your den has back-door escape holes. Besides, you collect lots of other stuff, too: bones, twigs, hardened scat left by larger mammals, what's left of an Anasazi sandal, potsherd, anything likely to bulk up your midden.

As to diet, you don't eat high on the hog. In fact, you're vegetarian. Your fare—if, for example, you happen to be a packrat of the *Neotoma stephensi* species—is pretty much juniper and little else, making you a "dietary specialist" to a degree uncommon among North American mammals. Sometimes you even choose a juniper's root system as den site. If, on the other hand, you're a Mojave Desert packrat, *Neotoma lepida* being among them, you repeatedly dine on creosote instead. Since both juniper and creosote have evolved obnoxious flavors as their defense against being nibbled on, you survive by settling for stuff few other animals can stomach. Not only are your juniper meals pungent with terpenoids, but they put you about as low on the food chain as any mammal can get because juniper twigs just barely qualify as nutrition. So while hiding out from coyotes and dodging owl-swoops, you go through life under the added burden of chronic energy stress. That factor alone makes your home-in-the-rock all the more vital.

Beyond defense against getting chomped on, a good midden, like the passive-solar aspect of Anasazi cliff dwellings, saves body energy by maintaining a fairly constant interior temperature. Park Service researchers at Chaco Canyon have tested variations in warmth and chill inside the largest ruin there, and have found that Pueblo

Bonito's massive structure acts as a heat sink, thereby preventing much change up or down the thermometer year-round.

Thus if you *were* a packrat, your midden's "thermal inertia" would surely keep you cozier by far in January than ambient air outside, yet also cooler in July. Nor would it offend your ever-twitchy nostrils that, in a really old midden, centuries of use by your ancestors have built up fecal pellets and congealed urine by the cubic yard.

We talking animals may find the very thought of packrats living inside "masonry" made of excrement more than a little bizarre. At the same time, we admit it's rather wonderful to think that such dens, built up over 20,000, 30,000, 40,000 years, now provide clues to the kinds of flora and fauna common to the Southwest all those centuries ago. Too, because packrats are compulsive accumulators, animal bones found in them allow educated guesses as to which Southwestern faunal varieties flourished or died out over millennia. For example, populations of the now extinct Shasta ground sloth are inferable from the presence of "indurated" or hardened scat found in several paleomiddens. Vegetation types, too, can be inferred by the presence of leaves, needles, cone scales, and pollen preserved many layers deep.

Unfortunately, there's no telling if a midden has been continuously inhabited. Radiocarbon dating isn't like tree-ring dating, able to pinpoint each year, season by season. Nor do packrats go in for the kind of living that allows prairie dogs and marmots to expand one family into a village or colony. Packrats aren't at all chummy — are instead pretty much loners, both male and female, except during mating season or when actively raising young. In their solitary lifestyle, of course, they contrast radically with the gregarious Anasazi. A single packrat may be so little attached even to "home" as to spend his or her solo days and nights in more than one den, freely moving into dens left vacant, shifting address from one night to the next.

What's more, the bonding so impressive between wolf mates and coyote pairs hasn't any parallel among packrats. The image of a female packrat fleeing a predator while her nursing young cling—or fail to cling—for dear life to her nipples bothers us. We'd prefer that she make a stand, putting herself between danger and her offspring, prepared to die nobly in defense of her sucklings (certain to perish if she does). But evolution isn't a tear-jerking journalist and cares nothing for our human fascination with futile gestures.

ऊ

Through painstakingly minute examination of these remarkable packrat habitations, paleobotanists have recovered evidence that Southwestern terrain of, say, 11,000 years ago was more montane than Sonoran, with forested areas of fir and ponderosa where today only desert scrub survives. But on the same evidence it seems clear that by the time of the great Anasazi developments, aridity had long since made Southwestern ecology what it is now.

Though useful to specialists, the rather tame picture emerging from all this delving into the proto-Anasazi domiciles of packrats is therefore far, far less surprising for its results than for itself. Yes, it's interesting to learn that during the Late Wisconsin period of glaciation (about 11,000 years ago) the Southwest supported more and bigger conifers, with a more diverse fauna roaming among them. But given all that meltdown of icefields northward, wouldn't we have expected as much? Less guessable, perhaps, is the fact that lots of what is now desert was also pretty arid then. Additionally, it turns out that the Southwest's unusually complex ecology has been complex for a very long time. That, too, is *mildly* interesting to ponder. Mildly.

For me, though, incomparably more mind-bending than any climatalogical picture these paleomiddens reveal is the startling fact of their very great age.

Ancient Greeks had a saying that certainly fits *Neotoma stephensi* and his cousins: "The fox knows many tricks, the hedgehog one. One good one." Through his durable proto- and post-Anasazi structures with their energy-saving thermal inertia, the timorous and lowly packrat has shown he knows more than any Greek or Arab or Native American about desert living. It therefore both amuses me and humbles our most grandiose historical pretensions to realize that dozens of the Southwest's packrat middens—some still in use—are incomparably more ancient than the Parthenon, the pyramids of Egypt, or the fabled ziggurats of Babylon.

Why the Southwest

Along with blood cliffs, blue buttes, dune-rippled distances colorful as an Indian blanket—Anasazi space, in certain areas anyhow, still stretches before us with hallucinatory clearness. That is, if we can see it. Like the Anasazi themselves, our Southwest is all but invisible to some eyes. For many, it's simply a wide-screen wasteland of "nothing there."

For others, it's an ecology of surprise, where arid life zones may flourish within a three-hour hike of flora fully montane. Great, soul-opening space, "weird" plant life, and blessedly fewer people make, by comparison, the American West and the East two different nations.

For ecology alone, take the Pajarito Plateau of northern New Mexico. One summer, as merely an instance, my son Nick and I broke camp there amid the yucca, cactus, and Apache plume of real desert. Walking upward at a leisurely pace, by late afternoon we had pitched tents beneath towering spruce and fir, then waited out a cold rain under an overhang, shivering in sweaters and parkas, only to crawl into our sleeping bags early, just to get warm. Our next day's trek took us back down into heat that made us want to stick our heads under a pump.

In the Southwest you can sit on a butte surrounded by square miles of parched shale and hardpan, watching how one narrow band of green meanders across it, then wanes: banks of a wash whose stream vanishes, swallowed alive by sand. Nights, under desert stars and the pull of the moon, you may need a down jacket while watching bats in their thousands smoke from a cave. Next day, on the morning side of the sun, you can fry eggs atop the hood of your car, gazing wishfully through the ripple of heat waves toward a shimmer-and-float of snow summits—the Uintas, perhaps, or the Manti-la Sals—barely above the horizon. If you're a Navajo, you can envy how clouds pour forth their blessings onto your neighbor's land week after week while you gaze at storm and sunshine all day but get, on your own land, no rain, just drama. Sometimes you get none all summer long. In a canyon drier than chalk you can be sitting, as Nick and I once did, by an empty gully that becomes a sudden hustle of pebbles and red paint almost the moment rain clouds let go. Meanwhile, you can count, high up, twelve separate waterfalls throwing themselves headlong off the opposite rim. You can watch rain blacken that canyon stone, then twenty minutes later notice how very quickly, as it dries, a cliff's earth colors return, fresher than before.

Everyone's prepared, of course, for how a desert's blossoming plants leap out of the ground after rain, but maybe not for how fast a dried-up puddle can fill, then seethe with copulating toads encoded to dig out and beget while the begetting is good. But as I've already said, in some eyes such wonders simply aren't there, because sight is equally a question of what we filter out and allow in. It's our personal way of being. As if what we see is what we are.

Reaching Keet Seel

Because tonight there'll be a half moon, you very much want to camp at the ruin. That means tent, food, water, sleeping bag, the works: meaning packweight—under the July sun of Tsegi Canyon. So what's remembered may fuse Keet Seel's cliff-nestled village, the best-preserved *large* Anasazi site in all our Southwest, along with those sixteen sandy, to-and-fro miles. Years after, the hike and that ruin may tend to become each other.

Ꭶ

Early-morning air, fragrant with the saffron yellow of prickly pear cactus, the pale yellow of cliff rose, the firecracker red of scarlet gilia, the purples and ultraviolets of penstemon. A clear sky's azure brilliance. Bossy squawking of piñon jays thinking this morning is theirs. For all the renown of Keet Seel's ruins, Tsegi Canyon itself seems reason enough to be here. And the trail's first mile is a cinch: a thousand feet down over sandy switchbacks.

Less than a hundred feet below, however, you note a mother/daughter pair backpacking upward at a pace like a reminder: what goes down into this canyon with bouncy stride must also get itself back out. Though only 8:07 A.M., it's already hot. The teenage daughter is, as sportscasters say, "struggling." Her tone to her mother has more whine than lilt, is even a little petulant, as if heat and weariness had converted the whole outing and the sun itself to her mother's idea. When you pass them, they're civil but decidedly unchatty, with minds evidently locked on unspoken words like "shade," "rest," "water."

For you, the sand makes a grand descent, is knee-easy.

Once down on canyon floor you follow Tsegi to its junction with Keet Seel Canyon, then begin creek hopping. Though most hikers prefer wearing sneakers, so as simply to wade the two-dozen places where trail becomes creekbed, you've a long partiality to leather boots and dry socks. Hence your stone-to-stone game of leaps and leg stretches to avoid wet feet. With each lurch your pack gurgles from its several canteens. Your Katadyne pump, a back-up item, would indeed screen out the giardiasis that Navajo sheep have added to the creek water, but the reddish-brown current would have you taking apart the whole apparatus to unclog a silt-caked filter every sixteen ounces or less. Then you'd have to reassemble, pump another pint, again dismantle it, and so on.

🌀

Four miles along and you stop noticing snake tracks on the sand of side gullies. It begins to be *some* hot. You've also quit delighting in how juniper sticks writhe, tons of them, so snakelike it's a wonder they don't crawl off as you approach. By now you're in a sand trench, an arroyo, carved by Laguna Creek. But its walls look rocky enough. You hurl a stream stone at one, whereupon a big puff of sand blows away on the wind, as if you'd heaved a grenade.

Round an umpteenth bend in the canyon you come upon a broad waterfall shelving down over a fault in the sandstone bed. You say to yourself, "If just the sight of it refreshes *me,* think what it meant to an Indian." Which serves as reminder: here, too, you hike into time. A time when the mind of Nature was entirely Anasazi.

A gliding vulture. So quiet. Nothing but fly-buzz.

Farther on you realize that if Anasazi children thought the whole world was made of red rock, they had plenty of evidence. You begin to believe maybe it is. A mile later, you know it. And no hiker trash. Interesting.

Another bend in the canyon reveals a flashing palomino, blond mane streaming. Then three other horses, sorrels. Then a couple of pintos. Navajo horses, all of them, whose reservation this is, with the Keet Seel site a national monument inholding. Horses prompt you to finally notice how close-cropped are grasses of the canyon floor, and how leafy branches on stream willows have been nibbled at. Cow flop shows there are Navajo cattle here, too.

Rock forms tower, left and right, in shapes so persuasive that nobody could live ten days in this canyon without beginning to feel, as well as see, they're enspirited. Their watchful, animal forms are plainly inhabited somehow, by something.

An iridescent knot of horse flies unties itself from road apples and buzzes apart every which way.

By six miles in, heat and fatigue have become parts of your body. Suddenly you start chuckling. Not at weariness. Not at the fiery sensation in your foot soles, nor even at the Fahrenheits. Instead, you're amused by your own curiosity, nagging at you for years: about reaching Keet Seel.

§

Four hours after setting out, you catch your first glimpse of it. Of just one corner of the whole cliff-sheltered village, but it makes your pulse quicken with the excitement of a Spaniard laying eyes on the golden city of Cíbola. The nearer you draw, however, the more a grove of cottonwoods blocks the view, so, by-passing the tiny campground, you cross the arroyo and head toward the ruin. Whereupon a comely young park ranger steps forward from a small cabin and intercepts you. "Nobody's allowed up there," she says sternly, "without a Park Service guide," and nods toward Keet Seel's rare array of still-intact walls. Scanning them, you try not to think it, but they are: unreal as a movie set.

"Yeah, I know," you explain. "I just wanted a closer look. From *here.*"

She's a hazel-eyed brunette, short and lean and very pretty, with a badge saying "Kathy Anderson." Her glare doesn't seem to believe you. Puzzling. No, more than puzzling. She's insulted your respect for Anasazi relics, for the Park Service, and is failing to read at first glance your right-minded character, your full quota of virtues. Besides, everybody knows about the guardian ranger who lives in a Park Service cabin among cottonwoods nearby. No exploring those rooms unless a ranger's along and so forth.

Does she really think you need to be told? And wouldn't anybody coming this far want at least to get a full first view of the ruin? From below, of course. At a respectful distance. And where else but near the base of Keet Seel's cliff? The better to admire how neatly, compactly the village's numerous room-blocks have tucked themselves under that long overhang.

"That's all I want," you explain, adding your intent simply to look—and from here, down below.

Her hazel eyes continue their no-nonsense message. Why is it she still doesn't realize that you're one of the good guys, not a vandal? Of course, every vandal thinks he's a good guy, too, all things considered; just as, conversely, every good vandal's some guy convinced that no Park Service clown in forest-green uniform is going to tell *him* what he may or may not do.

Checking the permit tagged to your pack, she reads its date and your name. By now her manner has softened, though not a lot. Born and raised in Ganado, she's worked here as a Park Service "seasonal" for the past seven summers. Come fall, she'll take off for the East, enroll at Syracuse University's creative writing program and earn her M.A., specializing in poetry.

So the two of you talk awhile about writing. As for reaching Keet

Seel, she smiles and says, "Believe it or not, some people actually ask, 'Why did the Anasazi build it clear out here?' As if they should've put it near an interstate!" Then adds, "If you want to visit the ruin, the ranger coming up to relieve me will be over at the gate later this afternoon. About 3:30. You can go with him."

"A Navajo? Young guy? Leading a horse?"

She nods.

You say, "Must be the one I passed along the way." An hour later, the last you see of Ganado-born Ranger Anderson, she's barefooting it through sand, leading that same supply horse, an old plug, down-trail, and leading herself eventually East. To write poems. Which you'd love to come across someday.

ⓢ

From your site at the tiny campground across the arroyo, Keet Seel looks like human existence condensed to a village. Its array of some 150 rooms and kivas sits maybe fifty feet above the canyon floor, in a "cave" or niche or rift about two hundred feet long. What haunts you is that wide expanse of sheer cliff beneath which it shelters, yet by which is threatened: a stone sky, impending, or a tidal wave heavier than anybody can imagine, poised there, to overwhelm the entire human story.

Though Keet Seel's builders were brief and few (an estimated 125 or so, even at its most populous), their fewness feels like everyone. A tiny, fragile town, tawny as an unglazed pot, "Keet Seel" is in fact Navajo for something like "broken pottery."

Years earlier you'd been told its rooms look freshly abandoned. "As if the Anasazi just left," your informant had claimed. "Maybe a bit longer, say, five years or so . . . but everything intact, just as it had been when they lived there. It feels really recent."

No wonder you had told yourself, "Keet Seel. Must see."

But now, having climbed long ladders up into its ruins under the guidance of Ranger Wilson Begay, you're soon aware that "just left" was more romantic than accurate. Abandonment happened by about A.D. 1300, and the effects of those centuries are plain: in the pallor of pictographs once vivid on the cave's back wall; in the cleaned-out feel archaeologists leave behind, once they've exhumed and packed every notable and transportable thing off to museums; and in collapsed roofs over a kiva or two. On the other hand, it's true that Keet Seel's original aspect hasn't been much tampered with by rebuilding in the name of "restoration." Hasn't needed to be.

True, too, walking room to room along the village's main "street" feels a little eerie. You can't really say why. Maybe it's the many tall, tall perch-poles still perfectly vertical: for macaws, whose exotic Central American plumage is known to have been much-favored and traded for by the Anasazi. What a gay racket, in that cliff-cave, their raucous calls must've made, when rooms and rooftops and small plazas teemed with people. Imagining the gaudy flare and subsiding of their tropical colors, you suppose the village must've flown its macaws proudly as flags. Those poles are time-blackened now, their tips empty, silent; and that's a bit eerie, too.

So is the absence of everyone, including, somehow, yourself. With the same hush pervading everything, except for a random clatter and splash of cottonwood leaves below. You focus a lens on jacal-built walls, on the inevitable potsherds, corncobs. On smooth grooves worn deep into a boulder by the sharpening of stone axes and edges. On the handprinted cave walls, their pictographs, near which your camera's shutter makes a slight echo.

Ranger Begay is especially well informed and is also interesting in his own right. His deep-brown Navajo eyes, olive skin, and raven-black hair contrast amusingly with his hip, yet often bookish, vocabulary. He spent five student years at the University of California in Berkeley, though in true Navajo tradition his boyhood was shepherding, and his meals were of frybread and mutton. On his father's long drives to trading posts were miles of bumping around in the bed of their pickup.

"They averaged a lifespan of about thirty-seven years," he says. "Of course, infant mortality makes that a little misleading. Average height was 5'4". Not very tall."

You point out that Europeans of the same era weren't any taller, maybe not quite so tall. And that peasant diets in medieval England and France, for example, were notoriously poor. Even aristocrats of those days were small by our modern measure. Keet Seel's Anasazi must have been at least as well fed—and a whole lot freer and happier—than most thirteenth-century serfs, ground down as those were by venal bishops on the one hand, while being driven hard by rapacious barons on the other.

Because you pause to linger over a row of three *metate* stones, a *mano* stone laid atop each, Begay mentions an article he once read on Anasazi dental problems. "It was by this forensic anthropologist, about corn grinding and tooth disease. According to him the average Anasazi adult would have eaten seven *mano* stones by the time he died." "Sounds likely," you say, shaking your head. Seven stones. All that abrasion on teeth. Small wonder the oldest hadn't much left but gums.

You're leaving the site, ready to climb back down, when you notice a pair of stumplike piles of . . . what? Each is about eighteen inches high, grayish as old cow flop, but can't be. Different somehow. Ranger Begay chuckles. "Human waste," he says. "Archaeologists study that, too, mainly for indications of diet."

Your eyes widen. Not with surprise that archaeology refuses to turn up its nose at anything, even delving into excrement (though that's a curiosity in itself), but because you've suddenly imagined the flies, the godawful stink. Especially in hot weather. An outhouse? There? But no, that's just it, not out: in. Smack amidst all their living spaces. You're dismayed. How *could* they? Having done a little romanticizing of your own about the heartthrob of a young Anasazi male as he eyes that one special maiden, you're struggling to reconcile young love with stench. Which, as you realize perfectly well, *they* wouldn't have noticed. All the same . . .

It's small consolation to know that residents of Europe's medieval castles might void into the moat and then feed heartily on the fish that had eaten thereof, and that Europe's medieval towns reeked like landfills with sewers down the middle. Nor does it soothe your disillusionment that studies of such centuries-old Anasazi waste reveal dietary curiosities; for example, that the Anasazi ate mice, and ate them whole, fur, entrails, teeth, toenails, and all, but never ate lizards, snakes, fish, or water creatures generally. Yet they would eat cactus with, incredible as it seems, those tiniest prickles *not* removed: those pesky, semi-invisible ones finer than hair, the prickles so hard to get out once imbedded in your skin. The ones today's Indians use fire to singe off, like pinfeathers of chickens. Ate them right along with the fleshy part.

Before climbing back down to your campsite, you take a last look at those grayish, stumplike piles whose mummified nightsoil had made you shake your head, then laugh at your own flush-toilet preconceptions. Bad as asking, "Why on earth did the Anasazi put their village clear out here?"

ᔕ

Melting toward sleep, you lie in your tent letting the day's sights develop, fade, recur, however they please; not like colored slides projected onto the back of a cave, nor quite like a pageant, but with features of both. Waterfall. Macaws, fluttering. Smoke-blackened sandstone at the back of Keet Seel's cave. Dried dung heaps, prehistoric, like tree stumps. The lone red potsherd among so many gray-and-black ones. More waterfalls. Creek water the color of its canyon. A five-year-old girl not visible but black-haired and naked all the same, watching her mother poke at embers under a pot. Most persistently recurrent—perhaps because most surreal—an abandoned doorway with, leaning nearby, a flat gray cooking stone whose surface still bore the heat shadows of four corn cakes; distinct, unmistakable. Had they been, month after month, year after year, a little family's daily bread? That family's last meal before leaving? One they're about to invite you to share?

Seven hundred years! Nothing you've seen at Keet Seel or anywhere has ever given the past so human a presence as those outlines. Nor have you ever felt so deeply how many seasons lay between.

Yet the oddity of it. In Europe, countless broad-shouldered castles, uppity palaces, great cathedrals, town halls, and temples had been built and then tumbled entirely to ruin during the seven centuries since cornmeal batter had last been poured out, four equal portions, onto that stone for cooking. In the same meanwhile, dozens of nations had vanished, while dozens of others had come into being. With a drowsy sense that time's survivals are strange . . . too strange for . . . your thought falls asleep before your mind knows it has.

Waking around 2 A.M. you crawl out of the tent for a look. Starry night—and how! Despite a half moon, fires of the galaxy are clustered thick as juniper berries. Barefoot on warm sand you blink upward at them, turning to take in the overhead sky. As much night as the canyon's walls leave open, that much the Milky Way spans like smoke. Only then do you grow aware that across the canyon, in shadow, float the rooms and low towers of Keet Seel. Ghostly. By moonlight that's indeed partly the feel, but not the main thing.

What you'll remember best and longest isn't rapturous or "enchanted," just that pallor of moonlit cliff high over its dark rift of shadow. Tucked into which the vague details of walls, houses—with the absolute black of their wide-open doors and windows—are ever so faintly visible, mainly because you've been up among them, know what you're seeing.

Not a sound. No breeze now stirring the cottonwoods. Nothing. Just you under a half moon, motionless in T-shirt and shorts, looking across a canyon. At all that work. All that hauling and building. All the communal hope, the quarrels, the envy. The festivities and harvests and terrible griefs. All that long time. And you there, alone, shivering a little ridiculously, empty of any big thoughts. Just standing by your tent, looking across, not really thinking anything. The half moonlight, the brilliant desert stars above that pale, pale cliff. The stillness. "Gone," your mind whispers, though maybe you actually murmur that, half aloud, out of your feel for listeners not there. "Long gone, all of them, all of us. Everyone happy."

Jailhouse Water

Inside something called nature, whose echo we are, I have found it possible to stand at a canyon spring in southeastern Utah and become a prehistoric desert dweller with no effort more complicated than thirst. I'd been looking over an ancient site now called, erroneously enough, Jailhouse Ruin and trying to imagine the lives of its people that long time ago. Hours went by. The sun blazed. I drank the last of my water, then, dangling my four empty canteens, I headed for a nearby spring at the foot of a red cliff not far off. Its flow fed an oblong pool on which broken reeds floated near the lush brim, dense with yet more reeds, succulent and green, as well as with willow wands and sopping tussocks of grass. How rich their whispers sounded as I pushed in among them. But despite being dry enough to spit cotton, I stood there a moment, looking down, while thirst made everything simple as life can be in this world, clear as that pool. Then I pushed more reeds aside and knelt. Filling the canteens, I thought of an old phrase, "the waters of life," and knew that red-rock spring was their fountain.

Hovenweep

LAND OF SQUARE TOWERS

Amid desert badlands just athwart the Colorado-Utah border at Hovenweep National Monument, it is the evening of June 21: summer solstice. While to us solstitial occasions mean little more than fair weather, the prehistoric Indians who farmed this area nearly a thousand years back made them the turning points of the year. And because each of their years, thus lives, took the shape of the sun's annual north-to-south travel, solstices—summer or winter—were vital in ways we barely imagine. Visiting Hovenweep makes that imagining easier. On the other hand, its designation as a national monument implies . . . what? Scenic grandeur? Traffic pullouts overlooking points of interest? No such thing.

Instead, the Hovenweep terrain is more forlorn than alluring, with human rudiments to match: an outlay of rubbled rooms and of square, Anasazi towers hidden in or perched on the rimrock of canyon after canyon, the deepest of them shallow enough to be ravines. To this remote and unspectacular setting have come others like me, some nine or so, each of us hoping to see for ourselves one of archaeoastronomy's fairly recent discoveries, an allegedly "calendrical" effect: to see, that is, how one particular beam of sunlight, entering through a slit, aligns within an ancient room so as to mark a "standing still" of the sun.

Just as with the similar effect at Chaco Canyon's famous Casa Rinconada, questions arise. Why can't I and my fellow strangers take the experts' word for such stuff? This "seeing for ourselves"

. . . why bother? If asked point-blank, we might fumble for words and end up feeling foolish. Or perhaps each of us supposes all the others have solid motives for being here, even while feeling unsure of our own.

Nonetheless, we crawl on all fours through two outer rooms of the ruin now called Hovenweep Castle, letting the grit of their dirt floors press into our knees, the heels of our palms. Finally, the nine of us—strangers to each other—squeeze ourselves inside the dusk of the last tiny room.

It's typically Anasazi. A stone-and-adobe box, roofed with juniper traves under packed mud. And typically small. Anasazi males averaged between 5'2" and 5'4". In fact, after Ranger Beth Pawlak and I led off, scrunching through the low entry too small to call a door, I had doubted that seven more could crowd in as well. Yet somehow they manage.

Outside, an orange sun a yard wide has lowered till nearly level with Utah's desert horizon. Out there, the occasional dwarf juniper will be slowly extending hundred-foot shadows even farther. Where they fall across grayish sandstone mottled by sparse clumps of sagebrush and serviceberry, they'll be lending its flat colors an indigo tinge. A tinge much needed, I'd say, because "Hovenweep," a Ute word for something like "deserted valley," seems a polite name for "ugly" or "useless." My own, non-Ute translation would be this: "badlands riven by countless junky-looking canyons often no deeper than a tall tree."

Did Anasazi come to this area for a last stand? Were they *forced* into these meager soils? Or had they perhaps deliberately chosen what nobody else wanted? On second thought, once upon a *very* long time ago, was something here worth having? In desert, that something is usually water.

The entire huddle of us, I suspect, shares at least a variant of that guesswork. Doubts about the tiny room we're in complicate our musing. Twenty minutes to go before sunset, but already we're concerned lest our bodies thus crammed together block the very rays we've come to observe. We're unknown to each other, yet because Hovenweep is reachable only across long miles of bad dirt road, often very bad, nobody visits on a whim. We know without asking that each of us has more than a casual interest in the prehistoric peoples who once farmed its soil—or what passes for soil.

By now, though, the sun's lowering amid desert silence has lowered our voices. We're expectant, subdued. I vandalize that mood by asking a pushy question only half shyly, "What's the big action in Anasazi ruins? Why aren't we all of us home, twiddling at our VCRS?"

For a moment, people look at each other. My breaking the tone of murmur and hush and indirection is close to bad manners. The humble fellow from Provo, Utah—unshaven, poor teeth, dressed in smudged undershirt and banana-yellow ballcap—says, "It's the history of it. You want to know about them people because that's what history is."

Yes. In a nutshell, history is people who were.

Or is there more? Clearly Ranger Pawlak has given this question almost daily thought. She says, "I guess maybe people are finding they miss spiritual things." She hesitates, uncertain how we might take "spiritual" and the like from a U.S. government employee, then goes on. "It maybe sounds suspicious to put it like that, but I think it could be they're turned off by how we've been living. They're looking for spiritual roots, they're saying, 'Hey, think of these people here long before us—and just look at what they've left.'"

I'd spent two days in such looking, roving among square towers and rudiments and rubble mounds by the dozen: Tilted Tower, Round Tower, Twin Towers, Square Tower, Holly Tower, Cutthroat Castle, among others. Towers round or square or both; that is, the west side rounded and the east side squared. Towers built on canyon rims, on canyon floors, even on boulders. The oddity of those, the boulder-founded ones, held special appeal. The boulder might be little more than eight feet across, and its upper surface might slant acutely. Undeterred, builders had coped with that slant by carefully fitting stone and adobe to every dislevel, until up from such an irregular foundation rose a one- or two-story tower whose dilapidation proved it had stood even higher. Stones long tumbled from it littered the boulder's base like fallen leaves.

Each tower, like a little lighthouse perched on a big rock, would've made its protective function all but self-evident if I hadn't known about the Anasazi fondness for towers generally. Still, according to the "defense hypothesis," towers protected seeps and springs at the head of shallow canyon after shallow canyon. Which figures. In desert terrain, the rights to a mere trickle can turn quiet men violent. But trickles and seeps defended from whom?

Possibly, as a worst-case version would have it, from enemies near as each other; that is, from effects of long drought that pushed each little canyon community in this wide Hovenweep area into desperation, and a readiness to clash with its neighbors. Maybe the Holly Canyon people raided those in Horseshoe Canyon. Some moonless night eight centuries back, maybe armed males of Hackberry Canyon went slinking along their winding canyon floor like coyotes. Maybe they assaulted other males defending the tower granaries of Holly Canyon. Maybe raids and skirmishes grew to be a way of life, thus provoking more towers in response. Maybe that—along with rain gods grown stingy—finally impelled everyone to pick up and head out.

We check the time. Still seventeen minutes to go. The ranger's husband, a lean man of about thirty-five with the pale brow but tanned lower face of an outdoorsman, says, "Mystery, too. There's a lot of uncertainty about the Anasazi. People are intrigued. It leaves plenty of room for them to wonder, find their own explanations. Because nobody really knows."

The spinnaker-bellied man from Grand Junction, Colorado, grunts assent. A bespectacled young MIT-type expresses doubt. Although he wears Navajo moccasins whose buckskin is so new-bought it's still creamy white, as is the pair on his wife, he hasn't gone native. He is too innately analytic for that, a doubting Thomas who wants to believe, yet doubts. As do I. Given our planet's precession, its periodic wobble on its axis, he wonders, how could peepholes built into walls ages ago continue accurate alignment with solstitial sunsets eight or ten centuries later?

At that moment one of us accidentally blocks the single solar ray penetrating this chamber—the ray we've gathered here to see. Instant hubbub of alarm!

"Oops! Sorry 'bout that," says the eclipsing body, and scrunches itself correctively before I can tell who. The ray reappears, a sun blob, oozing across the wall's rough-hewn courses of sandstone: hypnotic, as if a fate. A burning emblem about to set itself on an evening of our lives like a brand or seal. Interior gloom makes it a dazzle of orange fire that indeed all but smolders. It reminds me of solar rays that, as a boy, I focused with a magnifying glass on the kindling point of paper, fascinated when their minuscule sun began to smoke.

In fact, given the dust we've raised by our entry and present shuffling, this little sun does seem to smoke as it eases ever so slowly from one adobe-mortared stone to the next. Within its brilliance, a particular chunk of wall blazes then fades as the sun's self-projection passes on, nearing "target": our room's east corner, coincident with the upper left corner of the low door we've come through.

"They were obviously a hard-working people," says the big-city type in the navy blue jumpsuit. His fiftyish head is egg-bald, except for the sides. That gives him a tonsured look, sorting oddly with his semiheretical skepticism about solar alignment. He knows the walls and apertures of the room we're in had been laid out between seven and ten centuries ago. He, too, wants to believe, yet like me he mistrusts the current New Age drivel about Indians. Here he is, though, as absorbed as the rest of us in watching that small, captive sun draw nearer the room's corner. He knows it does so at exactly the slowness with which, outside in the desert evening, the real sun is all the while drawing nearer the horizon.

If he reads Ray Williamson's book on archaeoastronomy among Native Americans, *Living the Sky*, he'll learn that *stellar* alignments would indeed be thrown off by the lapse of ten centuries. But *not* solar ones. He mentions having driven up here from the great Chaco Canyon ruins in New Mexico.

"Amazing!" he says of Chaco. "Absolutely amazing—the size, the quality of the stonework! You just wonder what they could've done if they'd had writing." Clearly he's a go-getter who feels that given an alphabet plus a few breaks, the Anasazi would've been go-getters too.

I turn and in low tones ask the hefty fellow from Grand Junction about his visits to ruins along nearby Hackberry Canyon and Horseshoe Canyon. He denies having either much interest in or knowledge of Anasazi culture, yet it's clear that he has a great deal of both. Then why the disclaimer? Is he a professional pothunter who bootlegs artifacts, but who nonetheless has grown curious about the dead he steals from? Or is his a curiosity that he considers, reasonably enough, none of my business? Beats me. In the high Southwest, illegal pothunters abound. But then, so do Anasazi buffs.

Meanwhile, the ranger has begun pointing out a sort of auxiliary attraction: the six-inch slit on the room's southwest side. Though now in late June it transmits no direct sunlight, December sun will make its positioning another story. Precisely at winter solstice, it admits rays striking the upper right corner of a small door on the opposite wall. And yet more. Another aperture admits rays marking the equinox, far trickier to align for than any solstice.

Are such alignments mere happenstance? That's everybody's question. Beth Pawlak has just read the Williamson book. She says, "He worked out odds against those *solstitial* alignments being accidental. It came to something like one in 3,600. Plus," she says, "when you factor in the equinoctial alignment, those odds go up a good deal. One in around 200,000!"

The sun blob has oozed *almost* to the relevant room corner/door corner. Talk lulls, falls silent. By now I feel this to be one of the precious evenings of my life. Inside these walls, in this little room, with its far tinier door. Waiting. Waiting with flesh-and-blood others. And with others present, though not in body? Disbelieving in spooks, believing that "spirit" is atoms—thus dies with the body, *forever*—I nonetheless do sense another dimension. A kind of presence. Which of course isn't, can't be, "real."

Putting it that way, though, is evasive. We entered this cramped room with absolutely no links to each other. But our shared expectancy has become a communion. And more. We're filled by— perhaps even at one with?—the people for whom these Hovenweep ruins, alien to us, were home. Our "we" of forty minutes earlier has widened and deepened. Within a small, dusty room, eight or more centuries old, we've been touched. Touched by hands that lifted its walls one small stone at a time. We all but hear missing voices. Our hushed comments, our long silences, are charged, as if our dusk and stillness were now mingled with theirs, "the people."

"Maybe later," I tell myself, "I'll analyze it all away . . . but I don't think so." And I ask myself, "How often am I, or any of us, ever this profoundly *alive* to the human?" Rarely. Besides, when the deep moments come, "true" and "false" don't apply. Only gratitude. Briefly, we've half become "the people." We know it, and don't say a word. We know that as far back and ahead as forever is, we are all the living and all the dead. So be it.

Yet nothing much happens. Except, precisely at sunset, that dimming spot of ruddying, interior sun *does* touch the angle where two walls meet. We exhale more or less as one. "They knew what they were doing!" somebody says.

"Way to go!" someone else cheers in a stage whisper.

Then we all exhale a sort of soft cheer, for ourselves, the sun, the Anasazi.

§

Back at my campsite a quick whir startles me. Nighthawk, flirting past with nimble, quirky asides that catch twilight insects I can't even see. Earlier, hummingbirds had almost continuously fired themselves through my camp at their usual manic velocities. Not now. Nesting or perched for the night, all of them. No bird calls even. Not so much as an owl. Nor a coyote.

Though the desert's western sky remains luminous with orange modulating through vermilion to a still-lively blue high above, eastward from my camp the Sleeping Ute mountain has darkened in response to the rise of Earth's shadow. Well up in the southern sky shine Venus and Mars. They're unusually near to each other, a conjunction that astronomers say won't happen again for over a hundred years.

Their planetary radiance seems liquid. Is it because this evening sky feels drinkable? I think so. That, and the air's perfect calm now, contrast oddly with Hopi and Pueblo views of Venus and Mars. Hopi lore calls them the War Twins, and Hopi tradition claims descent from the Anasazi. If Hovenweep's hundreds of one-, two-, and three-story towers had indeed, as seems likely, been built for defense, calling these planets warriors might have come all too naturally. As for the towers, once abandoned, they took nearly a millennium to relax into the dilapidation we find so picturesque, so mysterious. By baffling our analytical bent, their rise and desertion makes the best kind of story, one we relish all the more because nobody's alive who can tell it. Which, as we sense, makes it our own story to come.

More truly perhaps than we'd like to believe. I think of a drunk I met years back, at Keams Canyon; he being Pueblo—Hopi, in fact—his avatars were indeed, in all likelihood, Anasazi. His glazed look bespoke a man from whom the will to live a difficult life as beautifully as possible had long since departed. As a Euro-American, maybe it would be none of my business that Hopi rituals, language, and customs are being eroded away. Not my affair, except for one thing: As one of this planet's talking creatures, I've a stake in any loss of beauty and intelligence amongst us. But such losses are something I'd rather not dwell on this evening.

Instead, therefore, I prefer noticing once again the real difference between the stillness of mountains and that of desert terrain. With mountains, it's busier, more active. There's always a stream or rivulet in it, however far at the back of the mind. Or some torrent's muscular rush. Or wind among pines keeping the inner ear busy also. Not at Hovenweep. The great, healing stillness here is motionless, entire. It asks for nothing, lacks nothing. If truly selfless prayer were possible, it would be this, now. A quietude so vast that two worlds float on it: our own and the world of once upon a very long time.

Flute Girl

Chaco again—and why not? Dawn coffee perking, others in the campground astir. On the grill of my much-traveled Coleman stove, the pot jiggles so excitedly, so full of pep and ideas, that its spout can't help letting off steam into desert air almost frosty.

Soon every ledge of this canyon will radiate heat, but just now my goosedown jacket feels good; however, twenty yards from my campsite a young woman, looking comfy enough in shorts and green T-shirt, sits cross-legged and upright in a cliff niche. I recognize her. The past couple of evenings she has sought out that same niche for playing her flute: shy, half-private notes whose breath sweetened this part of the canyon. Now, though, she sits motionless, a hand palm upward upon each knee, facing east with closed lids as, across the arroyo, the new sun's first direct rays glint over the opposite rim.

Chaco's wall of cinnamon stone at her back isn't high, sixty feet maybe. But it and the monolith chunks fallen at its base, plus the huge blue of New Mexican sky above and beyond, make her very slight indeed. Yesterday, while hiking miles on that rimrock overhead, I had stopped every so often to peer at fossilized casts or tunnels left in sea floor become desert stone. They'd been made by the prehistoric snail called *Ophiomorpha major*. Its petrified signatures looked like curved turns and oddments of rusty pipe that had once tried to scribble, back when all any sea floor could spell was slow motion: the Cretaceous period, which, in years ago, is three score and ten million. Which in rock time is nothing.

But why, on this clear morning, should some mental quirk put last evening's flute girl and those fossil vestiges inside the same thought? Because the slime trails or tunnels left by *Ophiomorpha major* do indeed look tubelike, that thought seems to have spanned the long ascent from sea snails to a flutist as so many segments of breath. Thus last evening, and the evening before, part of what the planet's great age has breathed into my flute girl, into her twenty-some years, got exhaled—however shyly—as those measures of soul we call music.

But what's she meditating on? Anasazi women, still here in spirit? Or on some spirit of place they, too, received emanations from?

Sipping coffee, I forget about her. From their jutting perches atop rimrock, Chaco's ravens have warmed enough to croak like broken pottery, which to ravens may be melody enough, no matter how "intermediate" we think it. Some flap clumsily into air, cawing as their wings stroke to and fro across this broad canyon—over its greasewood, its orange-red blooms of globe mallow, its wild rhubarb and thistle and saltbush—in level flights often rising no higher than a man. Every once in a while I glance sidelong to see if my flute girl has slipped back to her campsite, and seeing she hasn't, think, "Good" without quite knowing why. Since she's not playing, what's good about it?

It's as if her simply being there conferred a certain tranquillity. As if, in her feeling blessed, and surely she does, she herself were a blessing that makes even the coffee taste better. Merely the look of her closed eyes, her still, cross-legged posture, lends to my cup a touch of meditative contentment—a sort of second-hand, desert-morning Nirvana.

Up and Out

THE MYTH OF EMERGENCE

If you live long enough, you begin having days when it seems you may actually be getting some sense. How to act, how to see, what to care about. What truly matters. Perhaps your slowness in getting wise is simply what happens to people in a consumer culture, a car culture, a get-the-money culture. Subtle or raucous voices are always nudging, blatting, or sweet-talking at you. TV as obedience training.

"Wisdom" is a word it feels wise to hope you're walking toward, but with little chance of actually getting there. Arrival? That seems reserved for white-clad figures spreading both arms wide from a balcony; for hundred-year-oldsters, who from the front porch have seen it all by rocking chair; for gurus available in a six-cassette series from a 1-800 number; and for the gnomes of Zurich, whose wisdom is ingots softly humming to themselves in a vault.

Retarded as you may feel about having taken so long to get a clue, you've plenty of company, ancient and modern. Every ethnic group preserves one or another story version of much the same thing.

Pueblos, for example, speak of the Emergence, and for solid, archaeologically based reasons, it's almost certain the Anasazi did, too. Variations on myths of emergence, therefore, angle like spokes of a wagon wheel toward the same hub, whether those myths be local to Acoma, Jemez, Zuñi, Zia, Hopi, or other pueblos. As if in response to questions such as "Where were we when we weren't anywhere?" or "*What* were we before becoming as we are now?"

they tell of a sunless underworld from which pre-human beings issued. In the version collected by Frank Hamilton Cushing, who a century ago lived at Zuñi for nearly five years, these proto-humans were long-tailed creatures, muddy and cold, with scaly skins. Their bulging eyes blinked constantly, like owls, and they had webbed fingers and toes. An Acoma legend speaks of soft-bodied creatures imperfectly realized. Yet a different twist is given by the Hopi myth of subhuman "animals that somewhat resembled dogs, coyotes, and bears." Although they were furry-coated, their fingers were webbed, and their tails reptilian. Unsurprisingly, behavior of these less-than-humans was as confused as their bodies, including much violence, sexual license, and cannibalism.

All that was far back, in times murky as the world's beginning, and the beginning of us, followed—whether in Zuñi, Acoman, or Hopi myth—by ages of wanderings and migrations. But wandering toward what?

Not a "what" but a "where," which is also a more fully evolved body, a manner of traveling more upright than reptilian. Once there, your worries won't be over, but your phase of wrong turns and mistaken directions will be. At any rate, that's the goal. For Zuñi, the aim was to locate "the middle," and for Hopis, "the center place." Thus Pueblo myth is itself centered by one long "going toward," the kind that we call Becoming; the long, often-disheartening quest for the center. But aren't all our quests variations on the same thing, wandering toward the well-balanced, fully-realized self? Clearly it's an awareness of parallel evolutions—bodily and behavioral at once—even if we sometimes feel we've done more aging than emerging.

With the rise of Darwinism, a slogan using three huge words grew current: "Ontogeny recapitulates phylogeny," which meant that your growth from embryo to fetus to infant to child to teen to adult made you a capsule version of our species' entire evolutionary history. You were first a water creature, had a literal tail (the coccyx), and lived in darkness; then graduated into a little animal with an intellect so unenlightened it amounted to a cry and an appetite. You then crawled and gnawed, trying your teeth. Learned a first word, then another, then how to put words together. But hadn't yet learned to control your animal functions, much less good behavior. And so forth. Those Pueblo myths tracing "the people" up from mud, reptilian tails, and webbed toes into lawless conduct, then toward a final issuing forth into sunlight and right ways amount to variants of similar things.

The fact that some tribes of the Southwest place the site of their Emergence at or near the Grand Canyon hasn't caused me to claim I share that experience with them. As a non-Indian my sharing is limited to my share in human nature, but also to the mere happenstance of having emerged, literally, and on a specific afternoon, from the Grand Canyon's display of geological strata with my sense of personal identity forever changed. Except for that coincidence of place, it had nothing to do with Native American myth. Or so I supposed. It's just that to touch with your own hands and booted feet *some* of the depths of the Earth; to ramble for miles along trails half a billion years deep in time; to descend from there even further into time's actual abyss—well, that's like breathing human insignificance into your own lungs, of inhaling the brevity of your own bloodstream and muscle.

If, on descending, you're the kind of Grand Canyon hiker to whom that *can* happen, you'll never climb out of there alive; that is, the "you" who went down won't be identical to the "you" who emerges. In my own case, nothing before or after, seen or done, ever caused any change like it.

As if I were climbing the ladder up and out from a kiva's dusk into sunlight, which among living Pueblos is a symbolic repetition of the Emergence myth, that ascent from the Colorado River took me from my past as blue-green algae, then trilobite, then crinoid, then reptile, then rat, then ape, then *Homo erectus* . . . till finally I climbed out onto the South Rim of now. It was an Emergence whose stages were written in stone: from the Inner Gorge of Vishnu schist, up past Zoroaster granite onto Tapeats sandstone, over the broad Tonto Plateau and up again, past Bright Angel shale, Muav limestone, Redwall limestone—upward still through the complex Watahomigi formation, the Manakacha, the Wescogame, then rising through Esplanade sandstone, Hermit shale, Coconino sandstone, the Toroweap formation—with the final few, yet strenuous, hundreds of feet up through and out onto Kaibab limestone.

It altered my view of almost everything. It altered the way I now look into another person's eyes.

My knowledge of astronomy: why hadn't *that* wrought the same effect? Cosmic immensities, and all. It hadn't, and for the simplest of bodily reasons. Virtually everything we know about planets, asteroids, galaxies, and the like comes to us via printer's inks on paper, or colored pixels on a TV screen. Such knowledge differs greatly from what's gained while paying for it with rivulets of your own personal sweat, one downward, jolting step at a time, grunting slightly with each footfall. Does that sound anti-intellectual? Even at Oxford and Harvard, biology and geology students, to cite but a couple of disciplines, are told by their lecturers, "Well, now it's time for a field trip." The field idea was itself a boldly intellectual reinvention: for real understanding you have to get your nose out of books and go see for yourself.

So myths of emergence describe something like fieldwork: a whole people's "hands on," trial-and-error discovering of their place, which is also a lifeway.

As for book knowledge, it's true that before and after my personal Grand Canyon "Emergence" I had delved into technical studies of rock, sand, and Europe's early attempts at dating Earth's age. Naturally, what I learned went into what I saw, because seeing is done by the mind's eye. Bodily eyes are really the mind leaning forward. So even if the earliest humans had emerged from or near the

Grand Canyon, it couldn't possibly have been the same rim of Kaibab limestone I climbed out of and onto. Their seeing would have been a world different, on all but a single aspect perhaps.

That aspect, grandiose as it may sound, might have been the mystery of human existence. From childhood I have wanted answers to a few unanswerable questions, have groped toward them without ever giving my wandering, or "migration," any such high-sounding name as "quest." It's just that, without realizing what I was up to, I had simply never stopped asking myself, "What am I? Where *is* this? Why?" Surely those are everybody's questions, even if few people are naive enough to keep after them.

Hopi myth includes frequent admonition by spirit beings who scold "the people" for backsliding into low, lawless impulses and forgetting the meaning of life. Such forgetfulness surely parallels the "wanderings" of Hopi tradition and the "migrations" so pervasive in Zuñi legends, whereas "the center place" or "the middle" is as much how we live as a physical place. Call it a state of mind: the truest possible sense of who, what, and why we are. But whether any of the Anasazi priests or shamans, any of the Pueblo or Navajo or Ute holy men, ever got more than glimpses of such a mental landscape isn't for us non-Indians to judge.

Now comes the twist that makes endless questing for knowledge problematic. We assume that knowing what, where, and why we are is a good thing. Is it? When ignorance is bliss, the proverb reminds us, "tis folly to be wise." Despite such sayings, don't we claim to follow "truth" wherever it leads? Or is that only a flattering mirage? In medieval Europe and earlier, certain kinds of questioning were forbidden by authorities we now call benighted, repressive, tyrannical —which they were. That much we devoutly believe. Still, maybe the ignorance they promoted was to some extent "bliss."

Take genetic transmission of fatal diseases. If we had paid a microbiologist to mail us a profile accurately predicting, on the basis of genetic inheritance, our cancer chances or our chances of cardiac arrest, how many of us would at once rip open the envelope? While genetic markers are far from being specific enough to foretell anybody's death date, we might nonetheless agree there *is* knowledge it may be healthier not to have.

So just how fully into awareness dare we emerge? And at what cost?

In hundreds of versions the world over, one or another mythic or semihistorical figure looks upon a humongously powerful deity and is thereby destroyed by what he or she sees. Such tales imply that there's an ultimate level of awareness so awesome and terrible you can't stand it, a blaze of revelation turning to ash the mortal who beholds it unprotected. But what any myth or legend "says" can be variously interpreted. Influenced by my own "Emergence" from the Grand Canyon, my personal take on those death-by-divine-annihilation parables is this: There are indeed such awarenesses (calling them "truths" risks blurring into religion), ones which your old self cannot survive. If ever such light dawns on that self, it either looks quickly aside and forgets what it saw, or is zapped out of existence.

In the English nineteenth century, there were people who, on reading Darwin's *Origin of Species,* went into convulsions of despair, claiming that Darwin had "destroyed" their lives. If zapped, therefore, your soul's future depends on whatever was holding you up and together in the first place. Was it something you leaned on? False values? False gods? Even if what held you together was something like backbone supported by your own two feet, nobody who gets zapped by a world-altering revelation escapes being staggered. You could lurch into permanent loss of balance, cynicism being the worst imbalance of all. Alive, yet dead.

But why should cynicism have the final say? Without stirring a foot from wherever you happened to be standing, your zapped self may "emerge" into a world more strange for being more truly known, more mysterious—and therefore more daunting, even terrible—than the best-spoken among us will ever put into words.

What can't be spoken, of course, only a certain quality of stillness can express. That sort of stillness could be found in lots of
places on the planet, our high Southwest among others; but before
it can be found anywhere else, it must first be found in ourselves.
Only then, for example, would it be discoverable in the Southwest's
cinematic fantasies of painted rock and invisible air. In the butte-
haggard loveliness of its desolations, naked horizons. In its desert
wisdom. Which at certain moments seem to whisper, "You wanted
to know? Well, now you do."

Lizard, Hummingbird, Me

Among sights of the prehistoric Southwest, its longest, widest, and deepest piece of scenery remains, still, the least changed. Not only from what met Anasazi eyes as they first looked across it, or *down,* through a mile of clear air; its chasm hasn't budged much from what it was even before our species came into being. Though Anasazi ruins on both rims show four centuries of habitation, from about A.D. 700 till around A.D. 1200 (by which date they'd left the area forever), that presence of half a millennium is as nothing compared to time's visible abyss called the Grand Canyon.

Within it, four thousand feet deep, and basking on a red boulder big as a truck, is the tiniest lizard I've ever seen. Not two inches long, it must weigh less than a wolf spider; yet its glistening eyes are fully alert and lizardlike. On forefeet and hindfeet, membranes of mottled skin delicately web the splayed toes, whose claws are almost too tiny to see, while its tail tapers to a vanishing point. As lizards go, it must be *very* young. Along the spine, however, the skin's near-microscopic detail is mottled and wrinkled as a map of primeval time come alive.

Alive and blinking. How rich I feel, lounging here in perfect indolence, watching this tiniest lizard's occasional tail flicks! Otherwise, it's resting, too, momentarily motionless, forgoing for a while the skittery habit of its species: that fast-forward then freeze-frame way of moving.

The hummingbird that has already buzzed me several times does so yet again, and I finally get the message. Beneath this narrow overhang I'm scrunched under for shade, she settles down along the projecting stalk of a woody-looking something, where her finely woven nest perches tidy and small as an egg cup—which, as I realize with a smile, is what any such nest is. Her combative manner must mean she wants me gone because she's on eggs. That would also explain her many comings and goings, flying off briefly to feed, blurting back again—as she now does, fluffing and squirming on the nest, then rising, turning the eggs with her beak. Already in early May mid-depth in the canyon grows so Mexico-hot I've spent the afternoon moving from one skimpy patch of shade to the next, none of them good, so I'd say those eggs can't lose much warmth during her to-and-fro sallies.

Again she aggressively buzzes me, then flits off to a nearby piñon and chooses, always, the same bare twig. From there she throws me a reproachful look that snaps quickly away in the hyperactive style of her kind, but that's a hummingbird's natural magic: now here, now there, then vanished. No transition.

Her fast-lane metabolism reverses that of her reptilian cousin on the boulder. Extremes of the same desire.

Lie low and crawl, or fly and hurtle aloft? Grow scales or feathers? Long ago when they had everything in common, and poised at a fork in time's road, my minuscule lizard and this hummer chose between those opposite paths. Way back when. Before "before." Except heartbeats, all they share now is hatching into sunlight from eggs—and some reptilian skin, the lizardlike skin evident on any bird's legs. It's as if feathers, evolving from the top downward, still haven't got round to feet and legs. On some bird species, of course, that's not true; ptarmigans, for one. But they're cold-weather adapted, sporting such downy extremities, even the toes, as to have long ago lost patience with evolution: "Get a move on, will you? Our legs are freezing!"

Small as a droplet, that spunky hummingbird's heart and the heart (even tinier) of my basking lizard live at contrasting ends of blood's circulation, while my own far meatier mammalian heart beats somewhere midway. Such an evolutionary perspective might seem worlds distant from Anasazi minds, and is—but not *utterly*. In fact, it's by now almost too well known for words that the Indian's sense of kinship with the animal world continues to embody an age-old sanity that city living has stifled in most of us Euro-Americans. But that's changing. Annually more of us are getting the picture: all life is one. One rhythm, with near-infinite variations.

So here, a hot half-mile down in this stupendous canyon, three shapes of that rhythm are passing the heat of the day in each other's company. Inside more miracle than anyone can imagine, I'm the shape fully aware of three bloodstreams, pulsing, as if each heart were a hand that opens and closes on its particular share of life's blood—which it can never really hold on to, and would die if it did.

Is life itself something we must let go of to have? Metaphorically speaking, that's been my experience. The cherishable moments, many of them, have come via such realization: life is a thing-not-a-thing we're briefly traversed by. We're its medium, thus among its apparitions, true enough, but not its "message," and certainly not its possessors. So because we belong to *it* and not the reverse, I breathe most contentedly when I'm most aware of existing within life's magnetic field. "Yes, it's in me, all right, though just visiting . . . me among how many others, past, passing, and to come?"

In that mood I may also ask myself, "From the beginning till now, how many of us heartbeats have there been, ever?" More than our galaxy has stars? Far more, as I know well, but even dreaming such a thing somehow colors the idea of their number. I then imagine vast constellations of hearts far flung and free floating. Hearts of all species, appearing as innumerable pods that glow dark red. Galaxies of them. Each heart, dark at the edges, very; almost too dark to be more than faintly luminous, though toward their centers some appear ember-bright, and some like molten vermilion.

In my mind's eye, in their countlessness, they float but don't quite pulse, just seem to remember they once knew how, and once did.

The thought isn't fantastic. What's fantastic is the animal numbers that've so far been real. So here my own first-person-singular pulse is part of a trio, a "we": bird, lizard, biped. Three red-handed hearts, each in its rhythm, holding on, letting go. One, rapid as an adrenaline blur. Another, slow as ages of patience. And a much-bemused one, somewhere between.

Pots

Again and again I've watched an Anasazi youngster step from shadow toward a cookfire where a woman's hand is stirring something. Speaking a tongue I've no idea of, he always asks her, "What's in the pot?" But before she can reply, he dissolves back into shadow.

Sooner or later, if I dawdle long enough over a dark gray pot of the kind archaeologists call "corrugated"—the kind whose coils were pinched into their burred surface with the meticulous regularity of beadwork, the kind always fire-blackened at the base—that Anasazi boy's image takes shape without being summoned. Many and profound are our human interrogations of sky, of Earth, of each other; but does any question come closer to home than his: "What's in the pot?"

It's pleasant to know that even the earliest ceramics, whether from Europe's late Neolithic period or from Mesopotamia, often bear finger impressions that by their size imply feminine hands doing the making. Anasazi pots, too. Among modern Pueblos, pottery is a craft passed along the maternal line, daughter upon daughter.

A form of body language. If males symbolize themselves in chipping a spear point, an arrowhead, a knife, or even a scraper, women do the same differently. In shaping their conceptions of a nurturing vessel, they echo that ultimate vessel of human conception, the womb. At its crudest, the man/woman difference has often seemed to me, even when I don't want it to, simple as the difference between a knife and a cup: between to quell and to hold, kill and conceive. That's a distortion, I know, seeing only the worst face of man, best face of woman. But we can't help admiring powers we don't have, so as a male I naturally sense in the very idea of "woman" a long promised land.

Maybe that's why any potsherd I've ever wondered at under Southwestern sun has filled my body with an echo of the stillness it must've felt when yet inside my own mother. Over a sherd's gray-and-black slip, I may follow the tip of a yucca leaf brushing onto unbroken curvature the lines of a sacred design, watch the leaf-tip's chewed fibers trail black paint, watch a woman's hand guiding, pausing. Lifting and re-dipping her brush. Then slightly turning the pot as it was when newly alive, maternal and whole.

Of course, we humans didn't learn pottery the moment we first stood upright. Who hasn't drunk from the cup of his own hands? Though that hand-to-mouth drinking was surely the beginning of vessels, pottery came along only after we gave up our hunter-gatherer habits. Back when we were always in motion, we traveled light because we had to. Our receptacles were variously fashioned, but always suited to our wandering style. We used animal skins, gourds, basketry waterproofed with resinous ooze, but nothing so heavy or breakable as clay. Then, worldwide, wherever a people gave up life on the prowl, pottery wasn't long in appearing. Anasazi were typical. Slowly, as the craft of baked earthenware crept northward from Mesoamerica into lands of "the Ancient Ones," Anasazi cookery and diet improved. Pots, cups, bowls—in every needful and playful shape—were formed, fired, used, cracked, patched, smashed, abandoned by migration, buried with loved ones. Despite thousands exhumed, pieced together for museum displays by the roomful, incomparably more remain unexcavated, or got washed by runoff into arroyos, and from there into river mud.

Yet more have lain ever since near sites where they shattered, and in numbers beyond easy belief. Back in the mid-sixties, according to archaeologist Stewart Peckham, an authority on the subject, at one site alone an estimated million sherds were collected, sorted, and studied. At *one* site: a *million?* The mind totters, refuses to think what the total might be for Arizona only, not to mention Colorado, New Mexico, or Utah.

Because potsherds now stippling Southwestern sands imply daily meals beyond number, our own everyday hunger and thirst make it impossible to look at the humblest sherd without a sense of communion. After all, an Anasazi pot and just anyone's family share the same birth, each being made of clay and a woman.

Even so, reverence for our common humanity won't get us past the fact that the black-on-white ware most typical of Anasazi pots is an acquired taste. Admittedly, once that acquisition has been made, we may rhapsodize over a Chaco mug, say, or a whopping-big Mesa Verde storage jar, or a Puerco black-on-white olla whose painted lineations truly merit the term "eye-dazzler." All the same, what the loving eye sees in Anasazi black-on-white pottery isn't quite there. It's in a past we can't really know, yet try to surmise.

Alone in desert, to pick up a sherd from seven hundred or a thousand and more years back, then to heft its bit of clay pathos, turning it this way and that . . . is almost to remember having lived inside its lost language—one strange while since, one long time ago. When at last you return that bit of breakage to the sand exactly where and as you found it, your doing so is less archaeologically correct than simply the gesture your sense of its past seems to require. Each sherd speaks of a woman whose hands, most likely, had learned from her mother's hands: where the different clays could be found; which clays to gather for which pots; how to temper them with sand, or pulverized rock, with crushed sherds maybe, or even, lacking anything better, fibers of juniper bark; then, how to build up the pot's coils and smooth them; set them to cure before firing; thence to glazing, painting, and so on.

As I've said, our Southwest is strewn with so many millions of potsherds, I sometimes imagine the moon looking down on them as, with nobody to notice, they secretly reassemble themselves into a single flawless vessel no more than a foot high. It sits there; entire, perfect, weightless as moonlight. At times a sherd I'm handling may derive from that one unshattered pot whose wholeness implies a little circle of kinship gathered round it: all the living and all the dead, all the time.

The Road's Motion

Even at a standstill you can feel it inside you: the road as verge, as threshold, making "destination" a mere pretext for the real business of going to meet it. Certain words are like that. "Out West," for example. Pronounced even silently, they take the road all by themselves and, if you've half an inclination, take you along with them. The Hopi roved a long while, looking for the center place; Zuñi likewise, in search of "the middle." Anasazi wanderings, petroglyphed, spiral in toward a center: both a place and a discovery of self. But for many of us four-wheeled, non–Native Americans, isn't it true that our "center" and best mode of being is motion? Whose aim is less a place than simply the horizon.

§

Late July, 4:40 A.M. Plains of western Kansas. Across the pavement, a wheat field now stubble is still giving off the earth-smells of night. Miles distant, oncoming headlights from an occasional car or truck flare against a background of dusk. Though the sun's first glint over the horizon is a good half-hour away, that eastern rim is already orange, modulating to indigo overhead—with two or three stars so very faint, I'm not sure the growing light hasn't already dissolved them.

On three sides of the "Kountry Korner Grocery / Restaurant &

Truck Stop," a herd of big rigs, some fifteen or twenty, pulses and throbs, motors idling under empty cabs while their drivers order the biscuit and-gravy special, or maybe plain eggs, hash browns, and coffee. Walking among those mumbling diesels toward my car, I hear a very American possibility, one we can't remember not having, can't imagine being without: the road's ongoing promise— endless, auspicious.

In terms of waste, of pollution, we know a better way could be found. Just as surely as the bulk and chuff of each mastodon eighteen-wheeler feels already outmoded, we're certain a better way *will*. Because it must. Yet how could we fail to be expressions of what we grew up in? A U.S. of cheap cars, cheap gas, and roads going every which where. Haven't they made us a people most at home when making good time? Whipping past dinky towns like dull habits discarded.

Despite that pack of engines idly burning off foliage of the Carboniferous period, the early air is astonishingly clear, even delicious. In the waning dusk along I-70's westbound lane, headlights from the occasional onrushing trucker reflect off a green-and-white sign placing Salinas and Abilene straight ahead, Colorado beyond them. It's my way, too. Out of Illinois for a thousand miles and more, mountains and desert become my favorite directions. With dawn at my back, a full moon low in the west, well rested, undersides of the eyelids not grainy with fatigue, I ride the adrenaline rush of early-hour highway euphoria.

County after county my pickup pours me into a phantasmagoria of phallic silos, ditches where sunflowers flutter like windmills, fields of hay bales rounded like Iroquois lodges. Far below the easy equilibrium of high hawks, the plain rolls as if burrowed by some great, loam-shouldering mole. Sioux place-names appear—"Ogallala," for instance. "Oh, Ogallala! Ogallala, oh!" I pronounce aloud and laughingly often. Over miles of interstate, "Ogallala" insists on its syllables: a chant, a sing-song, a mantra.

Oncoming billboards loom, growing in size like imperatives: THREE MILES FROM THE LARGEST PRAIRIE DOG IN THE WORLD. Stuffed or alive, such a creature abides my visit to Rexford, Kansas. Which is the more peculiar specimen, I ask myself, that prairie dog or any animal called *Homo sapiens* who pulls over to see it? Then farther on, 20 MILES TO 5-LEGGED COW, residence unspecified, yet those miles pour past in no time.

With neither need nor intention to stop, I feel motion itself becoming my truest urge. Motion as essence, as life's very definition. Don't we say "animated" of things that move on their own? Of even drawn lines colored for romping across a movie screen. *Anima,* which we've borrowed to say "animal." *Anima,* which in Latin means "soul"—a gift we confer on the road through connotations in "highway," and which that highway returns by seeming to proffer us, its fastest,traveling vertebrates, more future than anybody can have. Diesel cab after cab, all chrome-glint and smoke, rushes toward and past like an explosion. Going west along with me, great double-trailer rigs high as the Wall of China sway slowly as they overtake my speeding six-cylinder truck. Animation: the soul of all highways? Road itself the Prime Mover?

Kansas dwindles, thins to its own state line, then is gone, as into Colorado I hurtle, scattering crows convened by a damp splat of fur-bearing roadkill. Soon, against a background of pine boards once painted but weathered now to a barnwood blue-gray, and in faded red or black lettering, hints at quite a story leap from billboard to billboard, with only a sort of meditation space in between: 8 YEARS OF STARVATION HAVE BEEN HARD TO ENDURE. Then a half-mile farther, BETTER TIMES ARE COMING. Another half-mile. MOM DID LET SOME GROW UP TO BE COWBOYS. And another. BEING STARVED ON MY OWN LAND BY MY OWN GOVERNMENT. And another. PRIVATE PROPERTY OR BUREAUCRATIC DICTATORSHIP. Yet another. FROM PRODUCTIVE CITIZEN TO BEGGAR THANKS TO BUREAUCRATS. And so on, to KING BUREAUCRAT VS

CONSTITUTION—thence to—ONE YEAR SINCE KING'S ORDER: "THESE SIGNS MUST BE REMOVED"—till finally, like a return to some opening F-minor chord—8 YEARS COLORADO STARVATION RANCH.

Beyond and behind that lettering, what's the sad upshot? Beats me. To learn more, I'd have to turn aside, wouldn't I, seek out that rancher or one of his neighbors. Impossible. The road's motion won't let me. "On," it says. "Farther." As for Colorado Starvation Ranch, slow adversity can occur only if we stop, settle down. Which is something the road never does.

🌀

To what extent do we fuel the road's motion by our desire to be ever so temporarily out of anybody else's control? Between one set of burdens and another, the road opens, keeps opening. We would not *have* to stop, ever. We could, if we wanted, couldn't we, pour westward past all obligation. Once we're inside the highway's magnetic field, the Pacific isn't there anymore. Nothing's real but good rubber, good shocks, cheap gas. Oh, smooth-cylindered American dream! To go, to go . . . so as to keep on going . . . into "on up ahead," where every come-hither smile and place resides, lacking only our arrival to complete them. Promises? Yes, ones that Western space goes a long way toward keeping.

Having just flown back from several months among the Alps of Italy and Switzerland, I'm in a unique position to say, "Ah yes, these incomparable Western expanses!" And say it I do, because having visited family, having picked up my wheels left for safekeeping in Illinois, I'll pause in Boulder only long enough to collect my backpacking gear en route to some canyoneering: first New Mexico, then Arizona, then Utah.

🌀

Scarcely big enough for a gas station, much less a town, Villa Grove's a place that at highway speeds you'd be into and past before you could finish saying its name out loud. Most are. It's on an arrow-straight highway down Colorado's wonderfully spacious San Luis Valley, so traffic shoots through. Yet from a back room the young woman tending its curio shop and restaurant and two mud-spattered gas pumps steps toward me wearing a cunning red sweatshirt: KYOTO.

"Have you been there?"

"Yes," she says.

As if in shared experience of Japan's most venerable city, our eyes meet over syllables sounding "Kyoto" and "yes"; no further word spoken. I leave realizing that with her in it, even Villa Grove isn't the boonies.

᠀

On the move again after sleeping beneath summits not far from Antonito, Colorado, I enjoy the fresh morning sun. Yesterday's wind-hoisted dust has been scrubbed from the air by the cloudburst that last night leaked somewhat into my tent, which is rare. Now the lower San Luis Valley's table-flat fields are full of a sky admiring its reflections off great sheets of standing water. The passing miles are clumped with rabbitgrass and sage, but in two-acre puddles the blue and snowy ridgelines of the Sangre de Cristo Mountains, already magnificent, are doubled.

With ten days to spend, nowhere to be, and no one to please but myself, already I seem to have diverted the expedition from backpacking to car camping. Years ago, a hiking buddy complained about my penchant for difficult outings: "You just have to suffer, don't you!" I denied it at the time, but it's true. I've spend decades making mere strenuousness a virtue, "valorizing" life with the joys of physical misery. Now, alone on the road, I decide to table canyoneering awhile. My new plan is not to have one.

For the first time in my goal-dominated existence, I somehow have received permission to go no place in particular. Up to this moment, my character has made such an idea impossible to think. Somehow my inner censor, some glandular secretion promoting aimfulness, wouldn't let that thought occur. Suddenly it has—and feels subversive as genius.

Immediately I begin to find myself an interesting companion in at least one respect: no telling where I'll head next. The moment I choose Farmington and Aztec, New Mexico, over Window Rock, Arizona, the latter route becomes a regret. Speeding away from Window Rock, I sense that the highway leading there would've been filled with all the interest my Farmington route is about to lack. So turn around I do, and drive again into montane uplands leading toward Window Rock. But not for many miles. Pulled onto the shoulder, I rethink my change of direction, heading through sandy desert and rabbit brush toward Farmington. High sun gleams off a raven's gun-metal wing, flapping for a while right alongside my pickup. Do I know my own mind?

Maybe so, but if so, I'm often the last one to know it. Letting the road's intuition decide for me—not once or twice, but many times—I begin to understand the West's ongoing wide-openness. Indeed, its allure is getting the better of me. "*From* here!" could, I discover, become an addiction blurring into a destiny. Meanwhile, overhead, a New Mexican cloud-blossom sky offers cumulus puffs whose tinted underbellies reflect the red land, and whose shape-shifting imitates my self-knowledge.

§

Waking, a nameless torpor finds himself using concrete slab as a mattress. Where? Some sort of open-air shelter? Under sky with cottonwood fluff filling the air like white spiders. Slowly the stunned creature recovers his first-person singular, then remembers being me: at a rest area off I-40, where an incessant east-west hustle of trucking grazes the north border of the Acoma Reservation, New Mexico, with the fast, night-and-day cartage of goods which most Acoma Indians (they, too, as Pueblos, descended from the Anasazi) remain too poor to own. "Lookee here," that round-the-clock, rolling insult hollers. "Lookee here, you shiftless, HUD-housed, big-bellied, booze-bemused, out-of-step redskins! Eat your hearts!"—as America's second-deepest belief, merchandise, goes whizzing past under their noses.

Between me and concrete, a backpacker's foam pad had made parts of last night something like sleep, even with the nightlong whoosh of truck traffic bustling through it. From a mile or so off, a big diesel's running lights had reminded me, half-conscious, of deep-sea creatures whose bodies emit blips of phosphorescence. At other times, those truck tonnages had seemed akin to Roman grain ships sailing to and fro the Nile Delta with Egyptian wheat for Rome's politicians to dole out to its plebes.

Atop the picnic table at the site next to mine sleeps a motorcyclist curled in a half-fetal position. Round back of that table's shelter, a guy, maybe twenty-eight or so, and a woman begin to stir. She pushes herself upright, looks about, doesn't notice me playing possum, observing. Kneeling in her sleeping bag she begins combing her hair, then steps forth in jeans and T-shirt. With a hand mirror, she applies eyeliner. Whereupon he rolls to one side, hawking and spitting before uncrumpling stiffly from his bag. Like her, he slept with his clothes on. As he busies himself in the back of their white Toyota pickup, I note how *very* dirty his sockless ankles are. Meanwhile, she sits at the picnic table with two books, one a Holy Bible, the other some sort of commentary.

On no evidence heftier than a furtive glance or two, I'm impressed by her determination that there be something more in her life than she has, something not made by hands. A stay. A pole star. She wants the world to be more than that big thing under their tires.

Does her hyper-grungy man treat her better than he looks? For the moment, at least, he doesn't treat her one way or the other. He is, she is. As if they've only that ratty pickup in common.

Plus a couple of sleeping bags and whatever's in the back of their truck? Which, like them, has seen its share. They're a breed I'm not used to. How many Americans live as if forever in transit? Driving all day and all night from Nowhere Special so as to be emptied back into their jobs, bone weary, at Nothing Much. And shuttling between that choice of regrets for how many years? The best part of their lives? Maybe the one place they're in charge, sole boss of what happens, is the road in between.

§

Gallup, New Mexico, is a mystery town. The mystery is why anyone not in jail would stay. Hock shops along Gallup's main drag offer Navajo silver, turquoise, and rugs. These alternate with package stores like cause and effect: pawn, booze, pawn, booze, pawn, booze. In fact, aside from Phoenix City, Alabama, Gallup's aggressive squalor and blatant rapacity in turning Navajos, Hopis, Zuñis, and others into alcoholics make it the most loathe-worthy town I am able to imagine.

Even in Gallup, however, one must have his morning coffee. I have mine at McDonald's. To my left an aged Zuñi woman in long skirt and head scarf lays out and smooths—one by one with the flat of a withered hand—each of three dollar bills while placing her order via a nine-year-old granddaughter, who gravely listens under black, black braids to a tongue I've no idea of.

Meanwhile, I sip coffee and watch a jovial, florid-faced septuagenarian—black Stetson, Levis, boots—carry two tall, frozen-yogurt cones through torrid heat to his pickup: one for him, one for his big old German shepherd. Inside, over in the corner, four middle-aged, Western-dressed males eating pancakes and sausage wouldn't rate a second look, if not for the heavy-set gentleman whose pant cuffs rise when he sits. On the side of his left boot I notice a small Derringer, its holster built into the boot design.

From the front counter I hear the Zuñi girl placing her grandmother's order, but in perfect English.

ᔕ

Compared to the erosional features of greater Arizona, evidence of vulcanism at Sunset Crater National Monument is geological news of fifteen minutes ago, but the chance to slip inside glass-gobbed tunnels through which molten lava once flowed is too good to pass up. I pitch my tent on volcanic cinder that, walked on, sounds like a roomful of kids munching peanut brittle.

For her nocturnal chat to us campers, despite wind, Ranger Billie Jean Holt has chosen to risk the traditional campfire, fitfully hearty, rambunctious. And what a night! Arizona stars thick as pollen! While she explains how eruptions and lava flows have made Sunset Crater special, red sparks whiffle away with each gust. From eye corners, we less-than-a-dozen campers share her preapprehensive glances. Blowing sparks are tracing wavy lines of red, undulant ones that fly, wriggling quickly off on the wind like incendiary sperm. Overhead, the pyromaniac galaxy that our planet condensed from, and floats in, surrounds our little campfire group with a universe. Quietly we listen. Sitting still, giving ourselves a break from the road, we forget about being whirled through the sky's wilderness of fiery worlds at unimaginable speeds.

ᔕ

Next morning, Arizona bridges carry me across river after river of flat sand remembering only the braided flow of gone currents—which is why, in desert, green is the same as snow. Never having been to Jerome, Arizona, I imagine wanting to go, only to find that I'm going, no idea beyond whim. Yet the noon highway bores me a little, so to liven up messages on road signs, I sexualize them as innuendo: LOOSE GRAVEL. FRESH OIL. YIELD. MERGE. When that palls, I count oncoming vehicles to learn how many look recreational, either because of kayaks on the roof, or tent trailers, or boats, bikes, what have you. The average seems high: seven out of ten.

Cool of early morning now gone, the cool of early evening yet to come, mid-August and mid-Arizona sun amount to a road awash in heat waves, through which oncoming tires splash toward me like power boats. The Fahrenheits mount, amounting to an hour of day most drivers would rather be off road than on. Yet again and again I see American spaces whose breadth redeems the shimmering floodwaters not there. Minivans crowded with families, however, don't even *try* not to look cranky as they pull up at stations saying ICE / GAS / BEER. Cars vie for pumps best shaded by canopy. When I brake or accelerate back onto the blacktop, floating ice sloshes in my own cooler like somebody shoveling wet gravel. In summer that sound becomes part of the ride.

"Human brevity" is a phrase any road through stone terrain *makes* you think. You can choose how you feel about it, but you can't help seeing that's how it is. Built visibly into Arizona's polychrome hills, into its arid dishevelments of vermilion butte and volcanic plug, odd as the logic of dream, is a past that's one omnivorous future: the kind geologists call "denudation." Theirs, yours, and the world's. Where the road ahead stretches through leagues of air surrealistically clear, over sagebrush broken only by piñon and juniper, you admire painted strata of pastel sandstone which that very air is helping blow away, so the price of cruising among erosional relics of two million years ago is your life as a puff of burnt breath.

〆

Heading north once more, past the peculiar, flamingo-and-camel-colored hills two miles south of Mexican Hat, Utah, I try the radio. Its tuner hisses through frequency after frequency. No receivable stations? Then a flow of spoken Navajo, whose mysterious veil lifts briefly with words like "Bosnia" and "Hong Kong" and "Clinton." I realize it must be the news. Then a Navajo-speaking DJ playing standard top-40 music, bubblegum rock. Ear trash. Then a program of Navajo chants, accompanied by a single small drum beat. Enigmas in every sung syllable.

Leagues eastward, the white and distantly visible peaks of the San Juan Range far over in Colorado remind me that a particular snowfall, turned to those ice granules called corn snow, might easily outlast anyone now alive. Our ephemerality. That, too, is motion?

Toward Moab, sheer cliffs rise like the Red Sea as dried blood. Red roadsides, red river. Grasshopper-greens of bunchgrass, bristling yucca clumps, black greens of juniper. Red signs alerting me to road crews. Then orange hats, orange vests, orange dump trucks. Then northeast on Utah 128, a winding, blood-red canyon road following the mocha flow of the Colorado River, with riverbank fragrance from tamarisk blossoms, all wispy lavender and fluff. A road sign—NEXT SERVICE 67 MILES—makes me glance at my gas gauge.

ⓢ

The Colorado's mocha flow must have put me in mind of lunch. I pull off the road at a picnic table near the water's edge, where a lacework of tamarisks with lavender blooms lend their fragrant shade, feathery as that table is solid. Its sandstone slab, a good six inches thick, bespeaks Utah's Mormon practicality.

Just as I'm chewing the last of my peanut-buttered bagel, up ride a young couple on matching Kawasaki motorcycles red-white-and-garish as the Fourth of July. She begins fishing lunch stuff from the panniers on his bike, while he steps into the tamarisks momentarily.

Being a loner doesn't keep me from talking to half the people I cross paths with. So I call over to her, "How hot does it get on those motorcycles?"

Her chin juts forward as she unsnaps her helmet, doffs it, shakes her brown hair into better order. She smiles half shyly, "Eet eez not hot. Eet eez yet cool air."

Her accent I can't quite place. I walk over as the man emerges from the tamarisks, his own helmet by now under his arm. They look to be in their early twenties. She, rather pretty, is a well-formed 5'2", her eyes lively under dark lashes. He's brown-haired also, though a few inches taller. And somewhat frail. They tell me they're from Paris, France, so—wanting to see the entire U.S.— bought the Kawasakis here when they landed. Not only that. Already they've been touring since April!

"Four months," I joke, "and still speaking to each other?"

She again smiles a bit shyly. "Oh yes," she says, "but a month uff that wass een Mexico."

"We go not fast," says her friend in an accent thicker than hers. "She cannot." His English is much more hesitant. "Hers . . . eez only a 350," and he nods toward the bike without panniers.

After roving the Pacific shore, they're now heading for the East Coast, but plan two more months for getting there. I let them know how impressed I am by their appetite for mileage. And by their stamina. "Well," I say, "by now you've seen more, lots more, of the country than most of us Americans. What's your impression so far?"

If her response isn't very original, she's nonetheless earned it. "Beeg," she says, exhaling the word like a gasp. "Eet eez so-o-o beeg. Also the wild*life*—we deedn't expect eet so much." He nods assent, then turns his hand to pumping up their tiny backpacker stove. Meanwhile, her afterthought adds me to the wild*life*. "Also the people," she says. "The people are vair-ry friendly here."

I'm about to wish them luck and leave when the novelty of two young and presumably streetwise Parisians in the American West impels me to ask how they like all that camping out.

Looking up from the stove, now lit and roaring, he says, "For me, I sleep okay, but she . . . " and he gives a sidelong glance at the woman. Her alert eyes lower, then meet mine with, again, that wistful smile. He continues, "Last night we air een forest, no? But she . . . she doesn't sleep so good. All night she eez afraid uff beers."

❀

Three miles past Cisco, once a cluster of buildings thrown up on speculation of oil underneath them, but whose principal business is now sag and collapse, an antelope poised on a knoll stops browsing, stares at my oncoming pickup. Oh, give me a home where the buffalo roam, and the deer and the antelope play?

Yes, but I mustn't get too uppity about the dissonant notes struck by that pronghorn and Cisco's abandoned future in oil no longer there, or perhaps not ever. Minerals are what my truck's engine is made of and runs on, which always leaves me of two uneasy minds about road time. While demanding my American birthright of un-limited mileage, I don't like knowing that every gallon I burn ex-hausts into the atmosphere five pounds of carbon. Yet burn it I do. If that isn't wanting to have the world both ways, what is? Dr. Jekyll and Mr. Hyde take turns behind my wheel, the one complicit in what the other deplores.

❀

"At speed" and heading back toward Boulder on I-70, the road loses me into its long daydream stretches. Past the village of Eagle, I en-joy the Colorado River jumping for joy alongside the highway; in fact, I'm happy for it. Half rock, half stream, its umbered waters are already hyperexcited about the long trip ahead, down into Utah, to join the Green, then through the Grand Canyon, and finally to the Gulf of California. Someday, maybe, I'll take that trip with it, go as far as the ocean. For now, however, the river and I are opposite forms of flow, and in opposite directions. Mere days ago in Switzerland I drove alongside the Inn River sliding eastward out the Engadine into Austria, toward Innsbruck, where a medieval bridge gave its name to a village now city. That Swiss valley of the Inn was a joy, but incomparably more so, this of the Colorado: open, untouched. If I could sing, my song, here, would be "Amazing Space." In all Europe there's nothing like our West's endless and pastel clarities. Oh dear American *lebensraum*!

I want to add, "And listen, all you big-city Easterners—stay there!"

But they haven't. In fact, I myself am indeed a stream in a stream. The river of vehicles I pass or am passed by abounds in out-of-state plates: Pennsylvania, New Jersey, Ohio, West Virginia. Lots of them on RVs. A pair of *big* Sportcoaches bearing California licenses seem tour buddies; each pulls a small sedan behind on a tow-bar, so as to have machines enough when they get there.

Similarly, the fancy-motorcycle buffs with their glitzy machines often tow small but glitzy trailers and often travel in two-person pairs, a husband-wife team astride each bike. Somehow I always smile to see them. At rest stops they seem so deeply pleased to be hovering over those snazzy, jukeboxed Hondas! I love them for being such fussy dudes about style; maybe they love me for my outspoken admiration of their rigs, which in gold-chrome gadgetry amount to a kind of functional sculpture. It's a bowling-trophy stratum of society that rides such bikes, the people to whom high school band uniforms seem "artistic"; and though I share none of their tastes, I enjoy their gusto. For them, more than for any of the rest of us, the road's ongoingness *is* their vacation.

Some twenty miles east of Glenwood Springs, Colorado, I'm stopped by the inevitable sign: DELAYS UP TO THIRTY MINUTES MAY BE EXPECTED. Ahead, a lineup of halted vans, motorcycle buddies, eighteen-wheelers, Winnebagos, camper-topped pickups, overachieving Volkswagen bugs, an open-bed truck hauling steel culverts, another whose stacked logs are held with great chains. They're solid for five, six hundred yards before curving from sight round the bend. I get out, happy to stretch. Already another several hundred yards of vehicle have accumulated behind my own bumper.

The old route through Glenwood Canyon hasn't for years been fast enough to suit people, but this canyon is one long scenic marvel of cougar-colored stone. Do those tourists in the biggest rush to put it behind them dimly suspect, via quick glances sidelong, that maybe nothing ahead will be more beautiful? Yes, the old road, a two-lane, was curvy. Yes, considering interstate volume, the route, I suppose, just had to be widened. Without irony, be it said that the finished result will have paid all feasible respect to the scenery through which it helps drivers hasten. Aesthetic and environmental values having been scrupulously weighed, this small, incomparable passage of our American West will be thereby degraded as little as a two-tiered, multilane, tunnel-boring, rock-smithereening intrusion can manage. (Till little by little it all is?)

Other motorists stand gazing around, half interested, half irked. A few toss stones at the river. A magpie gives its bronchial caw. Another replies. In vests and hard hats of Day-Glo orange, workers wearing sunglasses with mirror lenses talk into two-way radios that they pull from holsters like .45s. Out of drill-holes in rock ledge to my right curl little fumaroles, rising: rock smoke. Empty cartons labeled DYNAMITE litter the area. Sunlit conifers cling to outcroppings overhead, their evergreens enlivening the high canyon walls in which innumerable strata are stacked like old newspapers whose coverage tells of ancestral mountains drawn down to be sea bottom, then heaved up again to be riven by stream flow, and so forth and so on.

From the twenty-five-foot Pace Arrow RV in front of my car a gray-haired man in white shorts and varicose veins gets out, goes round back, flips open a panel on the side of his rig, and starts a gas generator. Which bugs me. Motors killed, I preferred the silence and river flow. As pleasantly as possible, however, I ask, "Why d'you need your generator on now, just waiting?"

He doesn't take offense. "Wife wants to put something in the microwave."

A guy in a very soiled chartreuse jumpsuit helps his buddy fuss with their spare tire. Half to himself the buddy says, "It leaks. The darn thing leaks. I wonder if it leaks."

Meanwhile, the humongous outlays of men, machines, and engineering that have been driving four lanes through Glenwood Canyon *over nearly a decade* amaze me. A blue crane one hundred feet high fills a pylon form with concrete. Another, farther on, is sole support of a platform hung from it by cable, while upon that platform five hard-hatted workers buck and shimmy in recoil as their pneumatic drills bore away at canyon wall. All along the route we've seen bright yellow scrapers, jumbo dump trucks—their very tires a house-story high; we've driven past linear acres of rigid metal triangles painted dull red; we've looked up at self-propelled, four-reflector racks of "Maxi Lights," each reflector wide as those used at ball parks. "Lot of round-the-clock stuff going on," we surmise, wondering how many hundred wood forms they've stacked up for poured concrete. Near them lie what look like several thousand rolls of roofing paper. And fuel tanks for reenergizing tired motors. And tall, cranelike contraptions, odd critters, clearly built specially for this job, but whose functions I can't guess at. While I very much wanted the canyon left as it was, I don't withhold my astonished respect for all that mountain-moving power and masculine know-how. Couldn't withhold it if I wanted to.

On a ledge overhead we watch a brave man earning good money. His bulldozer's right tread juts slightly out over a fourteen-foot drop. Now and then a tread-plate grinds chipped rock to smoke—a sudden puff of ocher—as he edges, maneuvering. Too little room for his blade? He eases back. Six inches. Nine more. Another three. If he loses it, he either jumps clear or doesn't.

"How'd you like to have *that* job?" a young woman asks her man.

"Might be fun," he says, grinning. Then, on staring a while at the skimpiness of the ledge, he adds, "No way."

From round the bend comes the "Whump!" of explosive, with dark smoke rising behind conifers. "A good powder monkey," says the hard-hatted worker near me. "He don't scatter rock." As the escort vehicle arrives with its flashing light-bar, a pretty flag girl waves us on up the canyon.

⑤

I'm barely back to cruising speed on I-70 when I come to a van with a canvas banner: "Trans-American Runner Up Ahead." While it pokes along behind, half on the road, half on its shoulder, with every hazard light flashing, the runner precedes his support vehicle by thirty yards. Passing with caution, I see a wan fellow of about fifty, grayly shuffling miles out from under his Nikes. He wears faded burgundy sweats topped by a white golf hat and, having committed himself to the enterprise, with a mere two thousand miles still to go, moves less like a runner than a medieval sinner doing penance for some abominable heresy.

Has anyone yet danced the polka across America? Has there been a trans-America hopscotch attempt? Sooner or later. In fact, I imagine the long, emotional planning sessions. At a kitchen table, an initially skeptical wife turns by degrees grudgingly permissive, then fanatic. I can hear the visionary tremolo with which the polka team or hopscotcher exhorts a support group. A local TV crew zooms its lens on official handshakes just before the gala, high-stepping departure of some state-champion dance-duo or hopscotcher. What élan! What enterprise! I foresee other eventual banners and vans: "Marathon Hand Springer Ahead." Or maybe: "Trans-American Terrorist / Expect Delays."

The fantasizing dissolves to real traffic. Riding windblown in the bed of a Ford pickup, two blondes sit as nonchalantly as if at home, while their long tresses blow like flame. Partly, anyhow, they *are* at home. Their fellow passengers are an easy chair, upholstered in buff and green, and matching sofa somewhat worn on the arms. For hours I'm passed by, or repass, that same Ford, the girls still there, a bit less relaxed as it begins lightly to rain on them and the furniture.

ఞ

By the time I've run alongside Vail's five or so miles of valley "development," have climbed to the summit of Vail Pass, then descended toward the Copper Mountain ski area, the road has left rain behind but has grown all too familiar. How many times have I driven this stretch? Had I never seen these snow-fangled peaks that abound on both sides of I-70, I'd be utterly rapt, absorbed into their magnificence. But, Coloradan, I say, "Yes, it's beautiful. It's what I'm used to."

Therefore, is one of the road's deepest-down appeals simple as difference? Or, in other words, sightseeing? I think it must be. The most miserly skinflint ever to rebristle a toothbrush has at least *considered* spending some money on what a few furlongs of new road might reveal, and the pleasures of motion. Which, illogically, grows to feel productive, like acquisition. Making time. Thus saving it. Accruing space. Out of what primitive impulse? Out of our dim hunter-gatherer past, when going ever toward the horizon was how we made our living? Velocity as enhancement: faster feet, better man. Even now, when instinctive atavisms put the pedal to the metal, do we distantly hear our hunter-gatherer ancestors murmuring approval of us as real go-getters?

Then, too, aren't all animals innately curious? Checking things out has survival value. Going to see what's over the hill, around the bend. Easier pickings there maybe, plenty good water, fatter roots, bushes more berry-drenched. Finally, can any urge of *Homo erectus* have been more habitual than the urge to lean forward—which is called walking?

In sum, do primal instincts partly account for what even our most personal roads are made of? Maybe yes, maybe no, and maybe no telling, but American space being what it is, out here in the West I'm certain of this much: far more than our European cousins we feel we belong where we're going, not where we are.

ᔕ

All the same, I keep forgetting you can't really *be* anywhere in a car. Only when on a whim I pull over to a dinosaur dig that the State of Colorado has lately opened to visitors, only when I have slid from behind the wheel, do I remember: for me, always, true knowing begins with feet. Begins with the particular crunch of desert sand and rock oddments beneath boot soles.

Before strolling a marked path along the various points of interest, I sip at a bottle of pop from my ice chest. Rumor of wind past my hat brim. Hush. Strong sun glare off mica-glittered "soil." The truce of no motion at all. Delicious. In it, the same wind soughing through the open weave of my straw Stetson makes a faint, musical note across the mouth of the pop bottle, a note that lowers as the pop does, after each swallow.

Though I'd hoped to see at least replica dinosaur bones, there aren't any, just shallow digs in the loose sand and chalky layers of mud shale. Nor is this mesa at all Jurassic looking, just nubbled with the usual sagebrush and juniper, and with the West's ever-present cactus and yucca. Various metal placards describing an inland sea and gone creatures tell me the customary Paleozoic stuff we all remember having forgotten. Yet just poking along from placard to placard feels immensely refreshing! Intense sun gives each shadow a hard edge. Only a few hundred yards off, the occasional whoosh of a passing vehicle seems distant and muted. Open sky, wide as the land itself, opens my life along with it. I can dawdle or go, have no place to be. Then I see a lizard eight inches long.

Its colors are ocher and turquoise and time. Its reptilian forebears standing sixteen feet high, weighing three tons. continue to exist within its shrunk body, a vestigial "then." I am a now. And a then. My human neurons have acquired the gift of putting me here when I wasn't: among blue mastodons grazing untilted horizons. In the midst of so much erosional detritus, any least glance, thanks to that ambiguous mental power, may turn retrospective; and in the American West, time isn't background. It's foreground, plus middle ground, plus lighting and props, and is, moreover, the show's main character. Who, wordless, has all the best lines, and will assuredly have the last.

So the tiny lizard is also life eras. Minutely, exquisitely scaled, its ocher and turquoise modulate toward the thorax's bright cerulean. But that little creature seen retrospectively grows huge, dinosaurian, gigantic. In this epoch-scumbled sand its ancestral shape now dims the hustle of trucks and RVs to a hum: one of big dragonflies with meter-long wingspans blurting hither and yon amid the fetid miasma over lush, tussocky swamp. And cycad trees. And omni-abundant fern thicker than light, back when time fed, then fed upon, then swallowed the Great Age of Reptiles—which time has hidden under my nose, there in a small lizard's glittering, iridescent hide. As I move slightly, this one skitters away, freezes, pumps once or twice, then skitters farther, onto a slab fifty feet from where the largest iguanadon ever found was lately dug up. Odd that I should have got here on fossil fuel from the Carboniferous. Yet really to be here, to know with my feet, truly to *see* where this was . . . I had to get out of the car.

So I ask myself, where does that leave me? Heading elsewhere, of course, home being only a sort of parenthesis in all travel. Besides, if anybody ordered me to stop hurling myself toward the horizon, wouldn't that balk my American heritage of its most tangible prospect? Well, perhaps illusions of destination are indeed the road's greatest gift to us, but if the road's motion prolongs that in-progress feel of becoming, pouring us through possible lives like water, highway speed does more.

It bamboozles the ego.

Even machine made, that sort of speed gets imputed to our inner selves as a personal excellence. Perhaps because sheer velocity fills our body weight with actual momentum real as physics, we mistakenly feel its power adding to our stature. If slow, we're mediocre; if quick, we're superior. Thus the faster the better.

Then, too, and especially when accelerating, we sense that we're staying ahead of the game. Otherwise, maybe we'd feel ourselves being ever so gradually overtaken, reeled in by something as vague as it is inexorable. Some great, omnivorous maw that pursues us without budging. Something that—to engulf the fastest person on the road—need never stir. Never has to move at all.

The Sleeping Ute

Seeing his profile after long absence, I've understood how you can exhale a sigh of homesickness suddenly retroactive. Whatever I had been looking for in other parts of this country, or the world, turned out in such reglimpses to have been nothing but spaciousness between me and the Sleeping Ute, whose indescribably luminous and Southwestern blue, greeting the eye across miles of distance, has upon each return made me feel, "I'm back."

That puzzles me a little. It's as if his whole region were more to me, strangely more, than just country I love. Presided over by a mountain like a man like a deity.

Though nearly ten thousand feet above sea level, its summit doesn't "tower." It reposes. That's so because it's the Ute's head, which, in silhouette with the rest of his mountainous north/south profile, does indeed resemble a reclining sleeper, complete with foot and big toe. His sacred personage seems all the more mysteriously meant by lying even farther than seven leagues from any other mountainlike form. So there he slumbers: lone, tremendous, self-entranced—and surrounded by the fairly level expanse of Ute country we Euro-Americans call the Colorado Plateau.

Utes differ in language and culture from the Anasazi bean farmers who once hoed and planted these lands, so the Ute way of looking at the mountain must be their own. Except in one aspect. So large and isolated a landform inevitably gives rise to the kind of story we call myth. What the Anasazi version was we'll never know, but assuredly there was one. Perhaps the earliest Utes migrating into the area had no knowledge of it. Then again, maybe they did. Maybe it came with the territory.

In any case, as Ute legend goes, the mountain is a god who became so vexed with his people he gathered up all the rain clouds in one mighty embrace and lay down to sleep. Any clouds hanging over the peak are ones that just happened to slip loose while he snoozed. But even a god can't be forever angry, so there'll come a time when he wakens from wrath and sleep and leads his Ute people to victory over their foes.

So much for legend. Geologically, he's a laccolith. That means his body's a sort of volcanic bubble: molten magma whose dome heaved up under a mile or so of sedimentary rock, which millions of years then blew and rained clean away till the Sleeping Ute lay open to the sky, breathing easy at last.

ና

Two months ago, atop a great mesa in southwestern Colorado, I spent an afternoon hiking in perfect solitude along rimrock high above the broad expanses of Montezuma Valley, picking my route past Gambel oak, serviceberry, the usual pepperweed with its sprightly white blossoms—and among or over tumbled hunks of sandstone. Though the mesa-top lay eight thousand feet above sea level, even in late afternoon dribbles of sweat kept blurring my sunglasses, did it so often I stopped stuffing my bandanna back in my pocket—just kept it in hand, mopping.

During one of my pauses to listen, I heard, unmistakably, the keen, piercing cry of falcons—a stunting pair of them! But by the time I got binoculars out and focused, they'd flown beyond my ability to tell peregrines from prairie falcons. To this day, however, it's another image from the afternoon that remains most tantalizing.

At an especially open shelf along that rimrock I came upon a small medicine wheel of loose stones looking fairly recently laid out. Its perfect circle was about twelve feet wide. Within it, crossing at the center, two equally neat stone-rows had been lined up along the cardinal directions: north/south, east/west. They also looked freshly placed, and must've taken some time in gathering, then setting so neatly each to each. But why? And why there? Perhaps because that spot, unlike most of the mesa's rimrock brink, was clear of vegetation: a natural lookout. Sixteen air miles west, in full view, lies the Sleeping Ute.

Had some living Ute's sense of the mountain's supernatural presence evoked them? That seemed even likelier when farther on I found another such wheel, this one much older apparently, with more than half its stones disarrayed or scattered.

🌀

Although my mailing address is nearly four hundred miles away, in northern Colorado, the mountain that's a man who is also a god has, each time on my again catching sight of it, moved me so reliably, so repeatedly, as to impart some idea of how—among Anasazi farming or hunting lifelong within sight of him—mythic powers *must* have become one with his shape. For miles and miles, anywhere you go, whatever you do, there he is. Inevitably, in the play of sunlight and shadow across his deific torso those Anasazi would have seen many a sacred implication. Even for people currently living in the area, his changing appearance centers sky and earth just as inevitably. Through the grand circle of seasons, from winter through spring to summer and back again, through red sun and blue shadow, the Sleeping Ute can't help becoming everyone's sundial, calendar, and compass.

Well, if our lives were half so fused with the spirit profoundly felt in our local regions as once were lives of the Cherokee, for example, or the Lakotas, the Cheyenne, or Utes, deep depression at being forced out of home terrain could kill us too. But that doesn't happen any more because, paradoxically, in our consumer culture a man's real home is money, whose other name is career.

If you were an eccentric billionaire goofy enough to imitate that ancient Greek named Diogenes, you could prove it, but instead of a lantern you'd carry a checkbook.

You'd simply wander around as he did, but in quest of somebody who wouldn't swap regions—and thereby give up the daily feel of ancestral terrain—merely because offered big bucks to do so. Somebody refusing to relocate for a price, at any price. In short, you'd look for a person money cannot uproot. Once upon a time, right here in the U.S., there seem to have been whole nations of them. Many. But that was then. Nowadays, your search might take a while.

Spirit Root

From its outset, our mechanized Euro-American and by-gone twentieth century has had one main aim: acceleration. So as to hurtle us into the next century sooner than possible.

Meanwhile, our love affair with fast-forward has begotten its opposite, a wistful primitivism, through whose nostalgias we day-dream back to a semi-Edenic era, one when lakes, rivers, and forests still had living spirits within them. Even as we hurtle, such dreaming is made all the more pensive by a hunch that somewhere in our species' banished past, its customs and rituals, lies our sole defense against progress.

We needn't only imagine. Right here in the U.S., a few of our fellow citizens, alive and actual, still dance to improve the rain. And believe. People of Second Mesa, for example. There on Arizona's Hopi Reservation, costumed as Katsina spirits, they continue ritual dance-dramas hardly changed since the time of Coronado. But not for beguiling tourists. They dance and sing for themselves. Their sense of this world requires it. Their sense of the sacred.

Theirs, not ours. We rootless ones, scarcely able to recall a single great-grandparent's first name, go back only far enough to regret.

ⓢ

My Anasazi quest, if I may call it that, had been set in motion by a chance encounter on the Hopi Reservation—rather, had been intensified by it, because gone time remains my lifelong fascination. So, once upon a twentieth-century summer (late June of 1984, to be exact) I was motoring toward a deserted version of Hopi prehistory called Keet Seel, notable among Anasazi ruins for being especially well preserved. Though the words "Keet Seel" aren't Anasazi but Navajo, and imply something like "place where a lot of broken pottery lies round," the proto-Hopi cliff dwellings they name were built before Navajos entered the Southwest.

En route to that trailhead all those years ago, I had stopped for breakfast at a little restaurant connected to the Hopi Cultural Center on Second Mesa. The place was so filled with Pueblo customers, I guessed its blue-corn pancakes worth trying. After all, Hopis are the people of the blue corn. Then, too, everyone working in the place was Hopi.

Sure enough, the pancakes were so delicious that when my waitress came with more coffee, I said, "Any chance of getting the recipe?" Never before or since have I asked for a recipe anywhere.

"Well," she said, "they have blue corn and egg in them. I know that. I've tried making them at home."

"But could I get the recipe?"

"I've asked them," she said, "there in the kitchen." Though all the cooks were as Hopi as she, tribal kinship hadn't swayed them. In a resigned tone she added, "They won't give it to me."

Not only the pancakes proved memorable. While I was eating, three lean Anglos trudged in looking like ditch diggers. They had scarcely settled at a table when another Anglo, a very large, white-haired gentleman, rose and walked out to their pickup, visible through the restaurant windows.

I had noted the white-haired fellow. He dressed like a man who meant to be noticed: on his left wrist he wore the flashiest bracelet of turquoise-nuggeted silver I have ever seen. His hands were drenched with rings. The bola tie on his chest bore an eagle carved and incised from turquoise so wide it was halfway to being a breastplate. His ample midriff shone with the Navajo conches embellishing his belt. Surely, I had thought, this man isn't just a collector, he's a dealer.

A minute or two after his bedizened person had begun snooping round the pickup's load of gray, barkless wood, the smallest of those ditch-digger types followed him out. Because I was leaving anyhow, I paid and went to my car, near enough for eavesdropping.

"I could see right away you had something special," said the white-haired man with all the jewelry. "Anybody could."

"We noticed you looking it over . . . so I came out," the grungy fellow said. His T-shirt and pants were clay-smudged. His gaunt face bristled a three-day beard of black whiskers. He looked both suspicious and weary as he added, "We're inside having breakfast."

All the while that hefty white-haired type with his silver-encrusted opulence seemed to accost the grubby little man, yet chuckled jovially enough. "Somebody gets near your wood, you come out, right?"

"You bet I do," snapped the other, as if his pickup held elephant tusks, which in fact the roundness and smoothness of its gray cargo vaguely echoed.

"How much do you get for it?" Apparently he was, indeed, some kind of dealer. "Say a twelve-inch piece?"

That "twelve-inch" business baffled me. It implied preciousness, whereas what I saw was a pickup loaded with snaky fence posts. Smooth, a bit sinuous, in lengths from six to eight feet long—just a lot of old wood.

"Twelve-inch?" said the grungy little fellow. "Well, no . . . we don't sell it like that." Then repeated the hint, "We're inside having breakfast." But that bejeweled fat man didn't budge. Instead he badgered the other for details: name, address, phone number.

Wearily, concessively, the little man reverted to the question of price. "Take eighteen inches," he said, "A piece eighteen inches long, like so . . . that'll run thirty-five to forty, depending."

I was shocked. For a length of old post? Up to forty bucks for a foot-and-a-half? At that rate the pickup was cargoed with gray ivory, all right.

But why? What sort of wood could be so special? Nothing kept me from stepping over to the pair and asking. Later I was sorry I hadn't, but at the time, that little guy's "We're inside having breakfast" evoked an image of his own blue-corn hotcakes getting colder by the minute. Besides, Keet Seel was still more than a hundred miles off, the desert sun rising higher, and I'd dawdled too long.

§

Long after my first visit to the Hopi Reservation, I now find myself once again driving from Chaco Canyon toward the oldest Hopi pueblos. Before climbing the steep road to Walpi, Sitsomovi, and Haano—the trio of villages on First Mesa—I pull aside at Keams Canyon. (The Hopi Cultural Preservation Office, while recognizing that Hopi has never been a written language, nonetheless suggests re-spellings closer to local speech than some previous versions of place names, with "Supawlavi" now preferred over the former "Shipaulovi." Of First Mesa names, "Sitsomovi" replaces "Sichomovi," and "Haano" or "Hanoki" is favored over the old spelling, "Hano.")

If you're browsing for the ultimate belt buckle as crafted by an Indian silversmith, you don't mind stopping here and there. When it comes to Indian crafts of high quality, Keams Canyon still rates four stars, even if a first glance around McGee's Indian Art Gallery shows little of that quality. Touristic stuff crowds the walls. T-shirts with silk-screened petroglyphs, Navajo "rugs" in miniature, Kokopelli ashtrays. The usual. Proving that where there's demand, there will be supply, even at one of the oldest trading posts in the Southwest. In a second room, however, you find walls lined with glass cabinetry (locked) displaying a not-so-small fortune in authentic Zuñi and Hopi and Navajo handicrafts.

What catches my eye on entering, though, is an obese Hopi in his early thirties. Neither his jeans nor black T-shirt gone gray at the edges set him off from hundreds of other bronze and black-haired males. Instead, it's how he studies an array of expensive kachina dolls. (Though "kachina" has customarily referred both to the spirit and its small carven effigy, Hopi speech distinguishes between the two by wholly different sounds. To mark the distinction, I use "Katsina" when naming either the spirit or masked dancer imbued with that spirit, but "kachina" when naming its carved and painted image.)

I wonder how come. Surely he isn't a buyer. The cheapest figure among them is priced at $3,000. From six to nine inches tall, they're the fancy, art-market kachinas, not whittled but sculpted; the kind carven in painstaking detail, with wood given the look of leaping sashes, of feathered headdresses, of woven cloth. Back in the nineteenth century, the post's founder, an Englishman named Thomas Keams, had collected kachinas by the hundreds, back when museum-quality artifacts were to be had for pocket change, or steel sewing needles, or a few yards of calico, or a pound of coffee.

Those traditional kachinas were carved simply, often with feet together and torso stiffly erect, whereas these dancing figures seem caught like colored fire in mid-whirl. By his motionless absorption before them, in his workaday T-shirt and jeans, that staring Hopi makes an odd contrast.

When finally he leaves, I examine the carving he had fixed on as if to memorize: a wonderfully horrific Nata'aska whose maw bristles teeth sharp as arrowheads, while his right hand brandishes a knife big as a head-lopper. On his prancing, uplifted left foot, the moccasin's buckskin fringe has been carved as if a-flap with that motion. The price: $6,500.

☙

Late evening. Over First Mesa a raking light from low sun steeps its strata of crumbly, rubbly stone in gold. More spectacular than any in the Southwest, its clustered villages—Walpi, Sitsomovi, and Haano—perched high on a thin spine, a dorsal *fin* of sandstone, would make anyone looking up there say, "My God!" On First Mesa the Anasazi are cliff dwellers still.

Hundreds of feet below those pueblo walls, almost invisibly one with the living rock, are small cornfields planted on sand. Wind tosses the widely spaced shocks of green corn, bushlike clusters of them, that at their tallest rise little more than knee high. Hopi cross-breeding has developed strains that grow low to the sand, and wind's incessant ruffling tells why.

But at the mouth of the road switchbacking to and fro upward, high as Walpi, I'm halted by a signboard: "Closed to the Public / Sat. & Sun. June 24–25"—for ceremonial reasons, as the fine print explains. Generations of Anglo curiosity have pestered First Mesa with visitors. The famous Snake Dance, of course, began drawing overflow crowds back in the 1880s. But as befits a people whose name for themselves, *Hopitu,* means "the peaceful ones," or "the friendly ones," Hopi religion is expressly open to all the world. It was so long before contact with Euro-Americans, back when "all the world"—far as the Hopi eye could see—was an open emptiness completely accessible to eyesight; an outlay of parched grasses amid rock affording rare pittances of soil; and outcrops that look into valleys filled with a wealth of destitution made all the more so, now, by ruinous overgrazing.

Yet the miracle of Hopi patience and hospitality continued, even though, as terrain feature, First Mesa has barely room enough for its own inhabitants. What with off-reservation Hopis returning on ritual occasions, it's no surprise that June's solstitial dances here need breathing room. The wonder is that First Mesa hadn't put up a sign fifty years ago: "Closed to the Public / Forever."

Thus with only an hour till sundown I put my pickup in reverse and decide to use the campground at the Hopi Cultural Center, just west of Second Mesa. Dances there are perhaps the most authentic of all. Then, too, like a pleasant kitchen smell, thoughts of tomorrow's dawn are enriched by ten-year-old memories of a destination breakfast.

ⓢ

Next morning, waiting for my blue-corn pancakes to come, I eavesdrop on a Hopi old-timer reminiscing in the booth next to mine. Eighty-five, he says he is, and a handsome oldster indeed, stooped only slightly by the years and the elements, with a full head of gray hair freshly barbered, and wearing a healthy glow on sun-burnished skin. His breakfast companion, far younger, sits with his back to me and says not a word. Just grunts once or twice while the octogenarian recalls his early days.

"You never herded sheep did you?" No answer. "Oh, that was hard, really hard. I was seven or eight years old. My uncle had a lot of sheep. Lots of them. Hundreds. You'd be out all day with them sheep. My uncle must've had two, three hundred sheep. I'm Sun Clan you know. There aren't many of us Sun Clan left. You'd be out looking for grass and water for your herd. When the coyotes came around I'd be afraid. I'd get into the middle of the herd and walk with them sheep all around me. I wasn't much higher than they were. Just my head and shoulders poking up, looking around because I was scared. I thought those coyotes might come after me. I was scared, but I felt safer with all them sheep around me. The hardest was lambing time. Oh it was cold, you know, that time of year. But you had to stay up the whole night and help the ewes. Sometimes a ewe would drop her lamb and just walk away from it. She didn't want nothing to do with that lamb. You'd be tired, but you had to find her, or find a ewe to put it with. Maybe that ewe wouldn't want that lamb either. But you couldn't just leave a lamb. Those coyotes would sure get it. You'd be cold and tired but you had to take care of all that somehow."

Again the younger man grunts. Assent? Boredom? Maybe to say, "Yes, that's how it is. Hard." A people who've survived desert conditions for ages are realists. You haven't a choice. In desert, you become either a realist or a set of bleached bones. Paradoxically, you also come into kinship with a world of realities the eye has not seen; a fact out of which, indirectly, the Katsina cult seems to have arisen in pre-Columbian times, as the great Anasazi centers underwent crises of mysterious origin.

§

Leaving the restaurant I hear a voice call to me from the parking lot, offering a kachina doll for sale. It's the fat young Hopi I'd noticed back at Keams Canyon. Seated in his Dodge pickup, he holds forth a carving: a Talavai kachina, spirit of "the red light at dawn." I like it. And the mystery of his earlier, transfixed staring into that display case comes clear. Like any artist, he studies the work of others.

"Two hundred and fifty dollars," he says.

His version of Talavai appealed to me by being almost opposite to those rather pretentious examples back at the Keams store. Talavai is usually shown holding a bell in the right hand, a spruce tree in the left, and I like this carver's subtle stylizing of the spruce boughs by tiny incisions echoed in the eagle feathers of Talavai's headdress. I like, too, the figure's repose. It suits dawnlight. In comparison, those pricier figures at Keams Canyon have bypassed tradition. Their art-market ambitions look hyperactive, as if dancing for dollars.

"It's very fine," I say, handing it back. "Thanks for letting me see it, but . . . I'm not a collector."

He sits there with wood shavings on the chest of his canvas

apron. His right hand fans at gnats hovering around his face (the omnipresent, pestiferous, Southwestern gnats I hate) then goes back to carving on a new figure just emerging from a blond length of wood. "It wouldn't have to be two-fifty," he says. "It could even be two hundred."

"It's worth the two-fifty," I say, and mean it. Maybe he cares only about making a sale, yet seems to hear by my tone that I do admire his work—and am not a prospect.

Instead of dickering, we talk about gnats, we talk about wood. He thinks the spring's big hatch of gnats has hurt sales. Gnats pester tourists so much they don't loiter over craft items.

I tell him how juniper midges were so thick in the forest northeast of Zuñi, they chased me out of a campsite. They go for the ears, nostrils, mouth corners, eye corners. Here they're bad enough, but not, as there, intolerable. As to wood, he says the cottonwood root—which is both traditional and well-suited for carving kachinas—is getting scarce. We talk about that.

🌀

Walking steeply uphill toward the highest plaza on Second Mesa, I hear chanting and drumming well before I see any singers. Hear the rattles, the bells, the heartbeat of their cottonwood drum, their unisoned footbeat. Then at the top I round a pueblo wall and see some forty or so fully costumed Katsina dancers chanting their dance in that tiny plaza.

Under the clear, pure, blue-sky sun of Arizona, they more than dazzle. Every turquoise nugget on their bow guards, every eagle feather upstanding from their red-painted masks, each silvery gleam off bells tied just below each left knee gives back its share of solar radiance, spic and acute as a spruce needle. Between the drum's beating and the beating of those virile, resonant voices, I am dismantled.

To be "rapt" is to be forcibly overcome by some power. By an Other. If by a malignant force, the result is rape. But if that power is benign, the self is ravished. Enraptured. Taken.

Expecting at best simply to "take in" a Katsina dance, my first-person singular vanished. Into where? Into them, maybe. Wherever, it was certainly out of myself. Not possessed—just wholly there without any distance. Filled completely with the vivid rhythm and color of one dancing plaza.

For the first few moments, therefore, I'm a nameless, addressless . . . what? An anyone. A Katsina dancer who is forty dancers whose one heart is a beating drum; a heartdrum, pumping into a footbeat that isn't a stomp. Far from it. Instead, a subtly rhythmic stepping in place. A unisoned motion going forward only as song, as chanted intonations whose sounds I've absolutely no clue to. Low and visceral. Then rising to a high, nasal humming, reedlike. Then low again, in broad-shouldered, deep-down tones. Oh, I'm going places within it all right, but because the chant's destination, its going forth, carries it all the way to where it already was, and had been, and will be again, I feel as if I were floating slowly around that plaza, inside its animal thrum.

In U.S. culture, souls aren't for sale unless the price is right. Then they are, almost all, especially to "the media." The Hopi soul isn't for sale at any price. This dance is it, is Hopi soul—or *one* of its apparitions—and is neither "a spectacle" nor "a draw" in even the remotest commercial sense. Moreover, an ancient Hopi prophecy warns that when Katsinas dance as mere entertainers, the Hopi way will have ceased to exist. Typically, therefore, this ritual is unadvertised, unannounced to any but Hopis, whose openness and courtesy have allowed me to look on.

Given the intimacy of a plaza barely long as a tennis court and little more than half as wide, it's plain to see these Katsinas are dancing for their own small village; at the same time, they are spirits dancing for all mortal onlookers, and the effect is a "we," a communion created by ceremonies my own culture has done its direct and indirect best to destroy.

🌀

Without question, my most immediate impression is one of intense, sunlit color. After the early black-and-white photographers like Vroman and Voth and Kate Corey, all cameras, all recording—even sketching—had been forbidden at Hopi rituals. Fast films never entered into the picture, to say nothing of Kodachrome. Often as I've pored over those pioneer black-and-whites, trying to colorize back into them the wild hues so impressive to the first Anglo witnesses, my imagination had added tints pale as those daubed onto a daguerreotype.

Gradually, my first, ravished impression gives way to noting detail. If I look long and well, if I listen well, maybe I can keep something of what I'm seeing, as if to have it by heart. Which I know I never can. Tethered to a ledge at the plaza's west end, preside a pair of golden eagles—male and female, judging by their size. They'll be honored guests till the Niman ceremony of mid-July. Well fed, their plumage glistening with preen oil, they seem only distantly interested if at all, whereas I'd love to borrow their acuteness of vision, their eyes with ten times the light rods of humans.

Impossible, though, *not* to recall each dancer's yard-long "tail" of fox pelt as it sways and bobs, nor the rhythmic surge in voices dancing to that drum as well as to their own very powerful yet beelike drone and hum. But later, recollecting the difference in kilts among the dancers, I'm certain to confuse their varied colors. Oh, I'm bound to remember this cinnabar red of the dancers' helmetlike masks, each with its symbolic fringe of red "hair" akin to a monk's tonsure. But will I remember even the eagle feathers rising from each headdress? And the burnt-sienna buckskin of the moccasin uppers, setting off their cream-colored soles? Or how the morning's breeze, here at the highest point on a high mesa, stirs into life the plump tufts of down feathers, cloudlike and dithery? And how the forty or more gourds, shaken exactly on cue, create rhythmic patterns making mere rattles dramatic?

The turtle shells rattling back of each dancer's right calf do the same, as do the tiny bells tied behind each left knee. On secret cues built into the chant, their percussive notes become the sound of rain, steady or intermittent. By late June or midsummer that's what all pueblos dance for: sky water. Not for cloudbursts tearing seed out of the sand, washing weeks of work into the nearest arroyo. Not for a few feeble droplets that begin, then stop, with the young corn left dusty as before. Nor, least of all, do pueblos dance for desert's cruel specialty, ghost rain, falling in those wonderfully generous veils of abundance that just miss hitting the ground. Rains that dry utterly up in mid-air. These dancing rattles are reminding the right kinds of rain how to sound. Enough . . . then none . . . then again. All summer.

Surely, though, I'll forget the wash of transparent white clay on the dancer's naked torsos, and the wavy lines smeared into it by a finger, lines standing for water; but not the bright ruff of evergreens round each Katsina's throat. In his left hand every dancer carries a tree symbol, sawn from wood and painted green, to go with the juniper twigs he holds in the same hand—as if to rhyme with twig-tufts of juniper bound to each dancer's knee.

Yet I'm missing details an anthropologist would pick up on instantly. And am aware that, in recollection, bracelets now glittering on each right wrist will little by little lose touches of remembered luster. So will the sweaty torsos, the leather pouches slung across them by a shoulder strap studded with silver. Nobody could forget the grotesque snouts and maws of the Katsina masks; however, their monster eyes may dim from bright reds and yellows and chalk whites to some indeterminate color, fading toward forgetfulness. Like all human history.

One thing I'm sure of. The power in this chanting and dancing and drumming I can never forget, with its vitality and brilliance, nor the elder who from time to time moves along the Katsina line. Dipping into a buckskin bag, his hand sprinkles pinches of corn meal on each dancer's left shoulder. Seventy-five if a day, he totters as he goes and presides, uncostumed, in a Western-style shirt of gray plaid above tan Levis. Yet round his neck hang several rich strands of turquoise, each "bead" a cylinder snug to its fellows, so the effect of each strand is solid yet lithe as a snake, thus rather appropriate to his role. He is the Katsina "father," whose task is to lead the sinuous lines of dancers into and from the tiny plaza, "feeding" them with those symbolic scatterings of meal, passing along to them the various petitions of dwellers here in the pueblo.

Corn meal. How many hundreds of mealing bins have I seen in Anasazi ruins? Small wonder that Pueblos of the Southwest call themselves children of Corn Mother, or that Hopi newborns receive a perfect "mother ear"—to be cradled with it, to be held beside it when, on its twentieth day, the infant is first presented to its father, Tawa, the sun, and to be kept nearby long after. "What your mother is, you are," say the Hopi. It's too late for wishing we Euro-Americans had understood our kinship to Earth half so well. Instead, at the heart of our trend-driven culture with its brief attention span lives an almost vandal envy of anything claiming to know what it is or where it belongs—an urge toward deracination.

In our entire population, are Pueblos the only ones left who know who they are? Individuals among the rest of us may know; or groups, networks of individuals. But how many of us know as a community, much less as a *people*?

Meanwhile, this Katsina dance and the Hopi religion it centers are already miracles of survival: hardy as blue corn, perennial as summer. So far. But the age of miracles is past. Not ages ago on First Mesa my guide, Maria, had told me that Hopi youngsters weren't learning the language well. In those days, nonetheless, I heard pueblo kids switching from Hopi to English and back again, unaware that they were. Now, though, the young people who speak it are, to my ear, dramatically fewer. In just fourteen years. What dies when a language does? How much of a world dies with it?

Almost to echo my thought, the Katsinas begin their dancing exit from the tiny plaza. But only to rest awhile, secluded. Then they'll return to dance another group of three songs. It's a rhythm that will go on all day—then the next day, dawn to sundown. For me, this rare continuity of Pueblo culture provides an Anasazi connection adding depth I'd been unaware of when first here years ago. Certain aspects of Pueblo living seem little changed from ten centuries ago to the recent past, and among Pueblos, Hopi ways have changed least of all. Here at Supawlavi, I'm standing so close to gone time as to be inside it. Prehistory alive in our midst and dancing. That's almost beyond astonishment. How many Americans realize? How many would care if they did?

Few could be made to understand how such a "quaint" pantheon of outlandishly gaudy Katsinas by the hundreds could be taken seriously, much less center a whole people. Despite labyrinthine variations in detail, the Hopi vision giving rise to them is simple. This physical world has a double: a spiritual world that mirrors it. Katsinas are the spirit beings corresponding to physical ones.

Are, in a sense, all nature made human.

So there's a specialized, particular Katsina for everything under the sun, breeding complexities that no single Hopi, however traditional, can possibly know. The fact that by age ten every Hopi child is initiated into the Katsina cult creates more than merely a shared experience.

Not least of its virtues is discipline. Gratifying as the performance may be for those in it, rehearsing songs, fashioning costumes, caring properly for (even "feeding") the sacred masks, developing the sheer physical stamina that Katsina dancing demands, devising comic routines for its clowns—all of that builds not only creativity. It builds character. Finally, Katsina pageantry eases life amid a harsh physical setting with excitements that are, among much else, just plain fun. In his oral autobiography Don Talayesva, a Sun chief born in 1890, looks back on an eventful life in both the Hopi and Anglo worlds and judges that his happiest days had come as a Katsina dancer.

֍

Whiling away the dancers' return, I walk to an overlook. On the steeply rising road below, Hopi men emerge from pickups and shoulder cases of soft drinks, then begin stepping slowly uphill with women who recrimp foil around pans of food the sun dazzles off of. One woman holds her toddler's hand and with the other totes a very new baby. The toddler balks and flops down, sobbing, but she drags him along with a harshness I've rarely seen among Indian parents.

All down the road of abrupt switchbacks, pickups and cars are now parked bumper to bumper, with more arriving. Every head of hair I look down upon bobs uphill with a raven-black sheen, upward toward these stone and adobe homes surrounding the plaza. Bringing lunch for the dancers, I suppose, because that's the tradition —food to be brought by women of the same clan as the dancers. Men have always been glad to see women coming toward them with eats; however, in this case there is a big contribution by one main male, the dance sponsor. He knows beforehand that sponsoring a dance is going to cost him. He's got to pay for that food. On the other hand, he gets to create the dancers' songs.

You'd think learning new ones on each occasion would be a strain, but Indian songs in general, whether Hopi or Blackfoot or Inuit, use plenty of repetition. And Hopi songs follow a few basic patterns already well familiar, so repeated elements ease the learning.

We non-Indians will never understand the great value that Hopi and Navajo tradition, to cite only the nearest examples, place on songs. We say, "Oh, he sold that car for a song," meaning a trifle. In contrast, a traditional Navajo might trade tangible things of impressive value for a song, literally. That is, in return for being taught a song, and thus for the right to sing it and benefit from its power, he might give turquoise, or a horse, or several sheep.

I know of one Navajo elder who in his final weeks spent days teaching every song he "possessed" to his son. In an oral tradition, that would take a while. It did. Close isn't good enough. The accuracy vital to a song's power requires that it be sung exactly as taught. And because the son's memory wasn't any better than yours or mine, he had to *work* at learning those songs. Touchy/feely nostalgia for good old Dad had nothing to do with it. To that young Navajo in a harsh environment, his father's songs were things of worth. They defended their singer against ills. They helped you overcome things. You needed them.

Near me, five Hopi children are running about, playing some kind of tag. The youngest, a laughing girl, looks about five. She cavorts and ducks behind parked pickups, hiding. Her enormous brown eyes peep from behind a fender. She then dashes squealing past the boy who seems to be "it." My comings and goings among them are far too superficial for generalizing, but I can't help noticing how Indian youngsters play for hours without the aggression and roughness you dread (and sooner or later *get*) from Anglo children. Earlier I had watched a cluster of raven-haired boys and girls horsing around with the same lively but unaggressive spirit. Hopi kids may be victims of rampant child abuse for all I know, and can indeed squabble, even fight among themselves, but these youngsters don't.

Only years after I began noticing those things did I chance across a study from the early 1940s on aggression among Hopis. In it a Yale researcher, Leo W. Simmons, noted that among those studied, whapping small children out of annoyance occurred "almost never," and that (as befits *Hopitu,* "the peaceful ones") violence in general was forbidden "to a remarkable degree."

Yet materially speaking, this pueblo's a slum. "Squalid" is too weak a word. Anything anywhere. Old mops tossed and left . . . for months, by the look of them. Flattened pop cartons. Cans, plastic bottles, bags. Bald tires and busted TV sets. The head off a motor block. A rusty truck muffler and exhaust pipe. Shattered hub cap. Dinette chair lacking a backrest, toppled near three splinter-edged scraps of oil-soaked plywood. The standard Anglo view is to explain that material goods in Indian cultures—except pottery and stone tools—had been biodegradable. Then came us, our metal, our glass, our plastic.

True enough. It's also true that Indians don't see things as we do. I know. Know, too, that when, a hundred years ago, Al Wetherill visited these mesas, he discovered that "you can smell a Hopi village ten miles off." A generation after him, Erna Fergusson, a student of Hopi dancing, nonetheless reported sufficient "filth" and "ancestral dirt" to keep swarms of flies "fat and well-fed." On the other hand, prior to sewers and plumbing, Europe's cities stank to high heaven. The stench rising from Michelangelo's Rome would have had us deodorized Americans reeling.

Knowing so doesn't change my inexpert view of Supawlavi's present squalor as a sign of mental depression. In fact, if a pueblo were a person, I'd suggest Prozac. Maybe that's exactly what the survival of these Katsina ceremonies adds up to: medicine, in both the Indian and Anglo senses.

ᕼ

Because poverty is written everywhere in this village, I'm puzzled. Why has nobody tried selling me silver or pottery? Or kachina dolls? Can it be that nobody up here at Supawlavi works silver or carves? No, not possible.

Quite a while back, miles from Second Mesa on a midday of early June, a Hopi girl looking nine or ten years old once stepped from a pueblo cluster of freestone and adobe and walked barefoot toward me. I had sat at the wheel of my idling Volvo wagon, noting her poverty—and that in her right hand she held a kachina doll. To offer for sale? I wasn't sure.

Nor had I been sure I wanted to be there. Oh, I *had* wanted to—but that was during winter afternoons back in northern Colorado, while reading about Oray'vi (formerly spelled Oraibi): "Perhaps the oldest continuously inhabited town in North America, founded somewhere around 1125 A.D." A town half as old, almost, as the Christian era! Under snowy, foothill mountains less than a mile west of my house, the very syllables of "Oray'vi" had sounded exotic as the lost Atlantis. My mind's eye had tinged its image with an aura of solar glow the more enchanting for having been first settled by Anasazi.

Once I beheld the actual Oray'vi of 1985, however, I was appalled. If ever some halo of ancientness emanated like a blessing from the Oray'vi of that Anasazi past, its glow had long since waned and gone out. Utterly.

What I saw was a low line of pueblo structures dim as dust, straggled around a much-littered plaza of hardpan and rutted clay. The pueblo's stonework was slovenly, its windows half-patched with cardboard or tin. What's more, except for the girl walking toward me, the place seemed deserted as Keet Seel itself. Even the doorway she had stepped from stood empty and black, no adult peering from within. Over that plaza, a June sun—made not of gold but white glare—burnt off every last fume of daydream.

Oray'vi the fabulous! Motor running, I had been deciding whether to go or stay when the girl arrived at the car's side. Now, many years later, I can't recall exactly what she said or how, only that I had sat there in an expensive machine surrounded by a poverty that accused me, tried me, and found me guilty. Probably that's why, when she thrust the kachina doll forward, I remember only her saying "fifty-five dollars." Which made me blink. But not just because the dollar of ten years ago had more clout. The kachina's workmanship wasn't much beyond my own casual whittling. To its white-painted figure a mask touched in with red paint, and yellow, and blue, and a few fatter strokes of black hadn't added allure enough to charm fifty-five dollars out of my wallet. Besides, as a man sleeping on the ground, eating on less than three dollars a day, I was probably aware how much gas fifty-five dollars could buy.

So I remember speaking my "No, thanks" gently as possible. Then repeated it. And repeated it again. Yet that barefoot girl seemed genuinely not to believe my "No" was a "No." Despite the midnight hair and Hopi eyes, the unshod feet, the faded dress lank and featureless as a flour sack; despite her few years and that bleak, tumbledown pueblo, she wasn't "fetching" nor as I recall even close to plain pretty. Just there. Her sales pitch didn't exist. She simply repeated her one question in a flat tone, not even plaintive.

Finally she did give up on the kachina sale, only to ask if I'd like to buy some piki. I had said, well, yes, I like piki bread very much but not just today—or something like that. Which felt slightly true. I do like piki. Even so, the scurvy features of the entire pueblo had left me disinclined to eat anything baked within its walls. No matter how hot the stone slab over which that blue-corn gruel had been poured, there would remain the handling. After the paper-thin spread of meal and ash had baked, human hands—all-too-human hands—would then have rolled it up into the traditional shape of a lop-sided scroll.

Now, after all that time, I remember clearly my refusing a brown-eyed, barefoot girl while sitting in a costly machine. I remember, too, why I hadn't simply given her a dollar, or maybe a couple. It had seemed, under the pitiless white glare of Arizona sun, that the whole thing was hopeless. A dollar or two would be demeaning. In the Hopi view of things it would make a beggar of her who hadn't begged but had offered me something of value.

So, discreetly as one *can* leave the scene of the crime, I had turned slowly around in the midst of "perhaps the oldest continuously inhabited town in North America" and driven slowly away. I can't really claim that in my rearview mirror I saw a barefoot ten-year-old in stringy black hair, still holding that kachina doll. Surely I felt too miserable to look. Only when remembering Oray'vi have I seen her there . . . ever since.

ᔕ

Amid Supawlavi's brilliantly sunlit junk and strewn oddments I suddenly notice some of that same gray wood whose value I had once found so baffling. A dozen paces off, three lengths of it lie nearly hidden under the chartreuse collapse of a baby bed. In turn, the flattened bed leans against pueblo wall whose stone courses have lost a surprising amount of their adobe mortar. Parts of each stone poke half-naked out from the wall.

Just as I'm estimating their own collapsibility, a vigorous old man steps from a door in that wall carrying scraps of black plastic. As he tucks them round the exposed ends of the wood, it reminds me once again of gray ivory. I step toward him saying, "Pretty good looking stuff you've got there." My tone hopes to imply I'm an old hand, sizing up cottonwood roots as any rancher might size up a horse. His intelligent eyes, the salt-and-pepper hair neatly cut above a finely wrinkled forehead, the impressively dark eyebrows not yet gray—all prompt me to add, "Are you a carver?"

He straightens and looks at me. Not a word.

After all, what business is it of mine? "I'm no collector," I hasten to say, "just interested"—which sounds dumb as soon as it hits the air. "Like your wood there. I was wondering, do you find it yourself, or . . ."

Or what? When not bugging them with our Indian-lover sentimentality, we Anglos have an endless supply of damnfool questions, thereby furnishing many Indians an ever-renewable source of belly laughs. Am I seeming as nosy to him as I do to myself? I imagine the trace of a smile in the fine crinkles around those intelligent eyes.

"No," he finally says. "A fellow I buy from brings it to me. It's getting to where you have to go too far." His face remains noncommittal except for those amused eyes under their heavy black brows. "All the way to the Verde, maybe even to around Winslow. It's got so you have to hunt out the wood. That fellow over there," he gestures, heading back inside, "he brings me what I need."

Across from me, under a black Stetson, sits a tall, thin Indian holding a can of orange pop. Legs dangling from the tailgate of a blue Chevy pickup, he sips while eyeing those two golden eagles tethered to their perch at the west end of the plaza. Like everyone else he seems to be biding time till the dancers reappear, and like me isn't with anyone. His purple-and-white Colorado Rockies T-shirt and his Nike high-tops show he's part of the TV generation, yet his tallness and build suggest not Hopi but Navajo.

Those eagles. Is he supposing they've been poached off Navajo land? Eagle-snatching by Hopi has fed an ongoing grievance. Last summer, in fact, the Navajo Tribal Council decreed that Hopi men have to start kicking the habit. From now on, they may gather no more than eighteen eaglets a year in Navajo territory.

Asking direct questions of Indians has never won me much of an answer. "Rockies fans everywhere," I say, smiling.

"Yeah," he says, "I guess so. I just like their colors."

"I kind of *thought* you might be Navajo," I say.

He laughs. His nation's appetite for purple velvet, purple sateen, has been a longtime love affair. By now my own sombrero of much-crumpled straw, my work shirt's washed-up blue, my scuffed boots, my sun-crinkled eye-corners—all seem to mute his heritage of Navajo disdain for whites. So I try my fake connoisseurship. "That's pretty rare-looking wood you're finding," I remark, and nod toward the chartreuse baby bed with its supplements of black plastic. Despite my "not a collector" beginning to be a refrain, I say it anyhow and add, "just interested." No reaction. "Wood like that," I say, "must take a lot of looking for."

His mouth corners move closer to each other. Am I a rival, hoping to learn where some good stuff is? And beat him to it? He decides no, I'm merely one more harmless member of the Indian-loving tribe, good for laughs if nothing else.

He opens up a bit anyhow. The cottonwood roots he brought today had grown well north of here in canyon country on the Navajo reservation. Only a Navajo knowing those canyons could find them. Lately a ruling by the Hopi Tribal Council had set a non-Indian licensing fee high enough to put Anglo wood hunters out of business, so he's doing better. For how long, he can't tell. As demand for kachina dolls rises, the Southwestern water table lowers. Demand didn't cause the lowering, of course; nevertheless, root sources are literally drying up. For decades now, cottonwoods have been dying off in arroyos or canyons where they once flourished. A generation ago you'd only have gotten one or two bucks for a running foot of first-quality root, say, eight inches thick. The same piece today could bring fifty dollars or more. Meanwhile, carvers multiply. And because authentic dolls are carved *only* from the water-seeking roots of that tree, usable wood grows harder to come by. Which puts wood hunters literally in the driver's seat, because the distances they must rove keep expanding.

He grumbles at that. "It's got so bad, now there's Utes clear up in Colorado getting into it. Hauling wood all the way down here."

My one direct question doesn't produce much. "How come on a day like today nobody up here at Supawlavi seems to be selling carvings?"

He shrugs. "I guess they don't want to."

ᔕ

Rustlings and shufflings from just round the corner hint at a reappearance of the dancers, whose song and color and motion will again enrich this tiny little plaza. Small wonder that early as a century ago Euro-Americans bought carven effigies of such dancers in great numbers. The missionary and anthropologist H. R. Voth managed to corral more than a thousand, and the trader Thomas Keams's private collection wasn't much smaller. Nor has demand slackened. Unsurprisingly, non-Hopi carvers have entered the picture. Even Asian sweatshops once got into the act. Prior to World War II, for example, Japan shipped a lot of *el cheapo* kachina dolls to curio dealers in the Southwest. Lately, the growing number of non-Hopi carvers includes at least one Native American version of those mass-produced Asian fakes. The Navajo Nation is not only unrelated to the Hopi but also legally uneasy neighbors with them. Despite that, I've seen a Navajo setup in which a young carver quickly roughs out the kachina torso and limbs, another affixes a head, a third incises one or two features with an X-Acto knife, a fourth adds painted detail, and a fifth Navajo glues onto that result a dab of cloth and feathers. Demand is such that even these assembly-line results, shrewdly advertised as "Authentic Native American," find buyers.

Can a Hopi spirit-figure be authentic if carved by Navajos? That's a question Hopi carvers naturally ask, but not one that buyers of cut-rate kachinas are likely to raise. Even less are they likely to care about mistaken details in a doll's costume and mask.

At the other end of the scale work those Hopi artists who have, yes, abandoned the old vegetable dyes in favor of acrylics, polyurethane varnishes, alkyd oils; who have even adopted X-Acto knives and Dremel tools; but who remain literally religious in their respect for every feature of the Katsina spirit their carving imitates. That old fellow protecting his cottonwood roots from weather—I like to think he's a carver of the traditional sort. Or arch-traditional maybe, like the Oray'vi chief Tewaquaptewa; in the earlier 1900s he purposely omitted certain details from his carvings, "so as not to offend the spirits."

Some Hopis deplore the sale of kachina dolls altogether. The dolls aren't dolls. Their Hopi names—*tihu* or *kachina*—don't connote "plaything." When ritually given by Katsinas, mainly to girls and marriageable females, that giving made each a kind of blessing, not a toy. A Hopi carver might therefore point out that only when a kachina is given by a Katsina on a ceremonial occasion is the doll "sacred."

A non-Hopi has nothing like a Hopi heart, not even wishfully, so I've no right to an opinion; all the same, the only kachina carvings I'd care to own would be those of spirits I believe in. Talavai, the dawn kachina, and Tawa, the sun kachina, come to mind. And maybe Masau'u, that primeval death spirit and fire spirit, hideous yet benign, so as to look like what's truest.

§

Early in their next three-song "set" the dancers are joined by the famous (or notorious) Hopi clowns who so greatly scandalized prudish Anglo spectators of our grandparents' day, and beyond. Especially when Christianizing do-gooders and their high-toned ladies were present, clowns delightedly mimed screwing with spectators, sodomy, eating of excrement, masturbation—strong stuff even now. But these clowns don't go that far, not this morning anyhow. They burst into view from a rooftop amid whoops of advice shouted to each other and then rollick down a ladder in the best, backassward manner of the Three Stooges imitating Keystone Cops. The last one pauses before descending, unzips his fly, and urinates into a gutter whose downspout, seconds later, sends its amber stream onto a well-dressed Hopi woman caught unaware below. She seems more than a little ticked off, though others think it's funny. Their laughter's a good omen. If nobody laughs, that's bad luck.

Bodies painted with yellow clay, six in all, their clown getups counterpoint those of the Katsina dancers. Instead of evergreens native to the Southwest, each clown sports "vegetation" laughably opposite. For ruffs of juniper, they use broccoli. Instead of a studded leather pouch, one carries a whopping bunch of celery done up in transparent wrap. As a necklace, for "turquoise" one wears a loop of plastic lemons, while a fellow clown is "bejeweled" with spring onions.

That visual counterpoint is carried into their antics. Whereas Katsinas allure by being otherworldly, the clowns are as down to earth as the dirt their bodies are smeared with. The Katsina motions are graceful and rhythmic, while the clowns move lumpishly as clods. The chanting Katsinas intone poetry, sung syllables; the clowns are, whether in English or Hopi, loudmouthed and blatant. The Katsinas seem like spirits; the clowns, oafs. A Bronx cheer. A raspberry. One long, loud, rude noise uttered by the backside.

With the eruption of these clay-bedaubed rascals, the dancers halt. Adding insult to injury, the six clowns then bumble along that halted line, aiming at each dancer a volley of questions and general mockery. Because most of their jibes are shouted in Hopi, I haven't any clue except gesture and tone. The dancers abide it all, motionless, stoic, "in character." Which is better than I do. To me the clowns *long* badgering of the still-seated drummer grows tedious, but then I've never been a Three Stooges fan. Plus, I'm not understanding a word of it. Meanwhile, chuckling Hopi adolescents to my left and right think the clowns' tirades are funny. Not uproariously so, apparently, but funny enough.

Brash and crude as they pretend to be, their comedy reminds me of Aristophanes, the great comic playwright of ancient Athens. He began his plays with the far-fetched, then piled on megahelpings of the simply outrageous. He loved showing how the body's most embarrassing needs undercut our soulful aspirations. In his play *Lysistrata,* for example, politicians make lofty speeches while trying to hide enormous erections. Unmistakably, these Hopi clowns derive from our very ancient sense of that human mismatch—the difference between sky and earth, spirit and flesh—making each of us an odd couple.

Clown counterpoint to Katsina seriousness sums up the Hopi world as a harmony of paired opposites. At Chaco's great ruin Pueblo Bonito, there's a literal wall dividing its complex of rooms, a wall whose stones were laid on a north/south alignment. Because many pueblos continue to this day their tradition of dividing inhabitants into paired "moieties"—the "summer people," the "winter people"—who in turn divvy up social and ceremonial duties between them, it's likely that the Anasazi did the same. Left hand, right hand. Such binary opposites, innate to our human habit of thinking, are as natural as (and perhaps rooted in) the body's symmetries of two by two by two. With our twin-hemisphere brain, we're of opposite minds about even ourselves.

Symmetrical as well is the Pueblo way of balancing each summer ceremony with a winter one. Furthermore, groups who'll perform summer rites meet in midwinter for preliminary rituals. Typically, for example, certain *pahos,* or feathered prayer sticks, important for the Niman ceremony in the blaze of midsummer, will have been placed on the sacred San Francisco Mountains during winter's darkest, coldest days. These are merely instances of the harmonic "poise" expressed by the Hopi, and by Pueblos generally, in playing off paired opposites. So the Katsinas intone and evoke what the clowns deride, yet their antics, being part of sacred ritual, are serious, religious.

In his autobiography, Don Talayesva reports his angry reaction to a bystanding government appointee whose horrified face had betrayed a narrow view of what's sacred. Talayesva, himself a clown at that dance, had said something like, "Well, white man, you wanted to get a good look, didn't you? But now you've ruined our prayers and maybe it won't rain. If this were dirty, we wouldn't be doing it.

This old Katsina dancer represents the Corn Maiden, and we have to copulate with her so our corn will grow and our people have plenty to eat."

"Maybe it won't rain." If your life depends on roots sucking moisture enough from desert sand, that says it all. During Talayesva's turn-of-the-century childhood, he was taught to wash his face with a single mouthful of water.

☙

For a better look at the clowns and dancers I walk round to the pueblo's south side and climb one of several ladders onto the adobe-covered roof, thereby becoming a nameless, faceless figure such as I've so often wondered about in the old-time photographs of, say, 1891. After dwelling on the page's foreground of dancers, my gaze has always been drawn to out-of-focus people lining rooftops high in the background. Odd to have become one; alive now and way back when.

That's truer yet of these dance motions, the resonant songs coming from Katsina masks amid the rainlike hiss and sizzle of tortoise-shell rattles, the bells, the pebbles inside dried gourds. Far from being unreal, the Katsinas have been brilliantly alive under this very sun for centuries. They're a past made ever-present by way of becoming the future. Or trying to. Despite heated insistence by Native Americans that Indian culture is alive and in no danger of vanishing . . .

No, I prefer not to finish that thought, prefer not to admit that my misgivings mean I already have.

So I turn aside to enjoy the stupendous view, amused by finding a few pesky gnats at even this height, but deeply moved when I notice the floating blue snows that mark the Katsinas' spirit home: the San Francisco Mountains, ninety miles of heat and distance away. Later this summer the Katsinas will go back there till the winter solstice, of common courtesy, we United Statesians should avoid implicit arrogance by insisting that "American" henceforth refer to virtually anyone in North, Central, or South America. Global usage even by bitter enemies of the U.S. has long since decided otherwise.

When it comes to offensive overtones, if logic had anything to do with language, "Pueblo" itself ought to qualify. As a word imposed by marauding Spaniards whose cruelties and exactions provoked, finally, the famous Revolt of 1680, "Pueblo" ought to be odious to the people it names. Yet because this one word says what only a descriptive phrase could replace, they themselves find it useful.

Logically, even the widely mistaken belief that "Anasazi" means "the ancient ones" or "the old ones" is fallacious. On average, women and men making up the various groups we cluster under the term "Anasazi" were younger than we are. Whatever negative spin it once carried—and may still for certain Pueblos—in current usage "Anasazi" now names the prehistoric peoples associated with Chaco Canyon, Keet Seel, Mesa Verde, and culturally similar sites. Names them, and does more. It now conveys rich and meaningful associations utterly absent from any substitute. Instead of an implied slur, exactly the opposite is the case. Overwhelmingly, in actual usage throughout the Southwest, "Anasazi" is so much a praise word as to honor Pueblos by association.

and will be given a send-off by the Hopi with a "going home" ceremony that will thank them for visiting these mesas, and remind them to continue favoring the Hopi way. Among innumerable different Katsinas are spirits of Hopis who have died and, in so doing, have "put on the cloud mask."

As cloud people they can often be seen hovering above those very mountains, or—in sympathy with their living grandchildren—may be seen drifting nearer, to bring their offspring rain. Generations ago Edmund Nequatewa, a Hopi Sun Clan chief, explained why newly bereaved Hopis tried hard not to cry on the occasion of a Katsina ceremony: tears would sadden the dead, who were certain to be watching the dance as clouds.

Five hundred feet below and for what seems a hundred miles in every direction, cloud shadows ease over desert whose aridities run through all the scorched tans of early summer drought. Glancing down toward an outcrop of sandstone, I notice a nine-year-old Hopi boy watching those same indigo shadows.

He's a lean little fellow in T-shirt and jeans, and stands gazing with folded arms, motionless. Does he too find the clouds' slow dapple and drift hypnotic? Morning breeze lifts the sun-blue of his black hair, cut just above the shoulders, but he doesn't stir. Does he share that traditional belief in cloud people? No telling. A girl—his year-older sister?—scampers over to him, turns to see what he's looking at, watches with him a moment. Then they run off together.

Earlier this morning the chanting and dancing had made Second Mesa feel like an island outside of time, but now its height and my rooftop view combine with those gliding cloud shadows to create a perfect illusion of motion. I'm aboard a stone ship steadily cruising, keeping pace with the drift of this far-flung cloud drama. Over that vast, sunburnt brown of desert plateau, blue shadows—the cloud people—keep changing outline as if forever spelling out one silent revelation nobody knows how to read. Meanwhile, in the tiny plaza, the drumming and chanting continue.

This view . . . I ask myself, "What if you lived up here? Wouldn't it make a mystic of you?"

If I were truly Hopi, maybe it would. For them, maybe it has. Maybe this desert immensity and emptiness do sooner or later fill you with a sort of inward plenitude. Maybe its endless revelation of *what isn't here* accounts for the Hopis being—as, in their past, they so indubitably have been—a virtual nation of mystics.

I think of that pensive boy, the little girl. Running off toward the new century? Maybe not right away, but sooner or later.

Had they been born less than two hundred years earlier, they'd have continued being hard to tell from Anasazi: dwelling in walls of stone and adobe; eating corn, beans, and squash varied by the occasional rabbit; living fully inside a solar year that centers this Hopi land, centered in turn by the Katsinas. They would have been poor, dirt poor most likely—except that in the kind of true community the Anasazi passed on to them, there could be want, or great scarcity, even to the brink of starvation, yet where scarcity is *shared,* poverty doesn't exist. Their wealth of inherited ritual would have made each circling year opulent with spirits and ceremonies. So they'd have owned, as we think of ownership, very little; but— once upon that bygone time—they would have belonged to everything.

Postscript: On the Term "Anasazi"

Despite its currency for the better part of a hundred years now, the term "Anasazi" has incurred disapproval from certain Pueblo groups. Not only they, but also Euro-American others reacting to that view, have, however, overlooked the obvious, as this note intends to show.

Pueblo objection to the term's Navajo origin is based, first, on the fact that Navajos migrated into the Southwest only after prehistoric Pueblo peoples had been long established there. Thus the Navajo Nation, being culturally and linguistically alien, had nothing to do with the builders of Chaco Canyon, Betatakin, Keet Seel, and other ancient sites. Second, some Pueblos feel that the original meaning of "Anasazi" insults their forebears. Both objections are logical "Anasazi" does indeed seem to be the garbled version of a Nava phrase. Worse yet, as some Pueblos see it, is the fact that "Anasa meant something like "old enemies" or "enemies of our ancestor

The Hopi, for example, now suggest replacing "Anasazi" wit word from their own tongue, "Hisatsinom." Current archaeol hasn't taken this hint, partly because phrases like "prehist Pueblo" or "ancient Pueblo peoples" are self-explanatory, but because Puebloans such as those of Acoma and Zuñi have their words to name the same forebears.

While ink has been spilt discussing logical fine points of t sue, a main aspect of language has been ignored: usage is ofte ical because words change meaning. *Logically,* for example,

Acknowledgments

Grateful acknowledgment for permission to reprint is made to the following publications.

"Up-and-Down Sun: Notes on the Sacred," first appeared in *The Georgia Review* (Winter 1995).

"The Real Surreal: Horseshoe Canyon," first appeared in briefer version as "Sandstone Spirit" in *The Rocky Mountain News* (May 7, 1995), and subsequently in its present form in *Under the Sun* (Summer 1996).

"The Tree Beyond Imagining," first appeared in *Dominion Review* (1996).

"Newspaper Rock and the Idiot Race," to appear in *Ascent*.

"The Pleasures of Ruin," first appeared in *High Plains Literary Review* (Fall/Winter 1996).

"Reaching Keet Seel," first appeared in *Pleiades* (Spring 1997).

"Hovenweep: The Land of Square Towers," first appeared in *Nimrod: International Journal* (Spring/Summer 1997).

"The Road's Motion," first appeared in *American Literary Review* (Fall 1994).

"Spirit Root," appeared in *Southwest Review*.